I want to dedicate this book to my mom and dad.
Thank you for always supporting me when nobody else would. I could always count on you guys to cheer me up and bring me up from the lowest of times.

I also want to dedicate this book to my mentor Andrew LeBaron. You pushed me harder in business than anybody else and without you I wouldn't be where I am today.

Thank you, Andrew.

I love all my friends and family.
Thank you to everybody who has ever supported me.

CHAPTERS 1-8

1- The Beginning

2- Starting a Business While in High School

3- The Struggles/Growth of Your New Self

4- The First Deal; Success at Last

5- Hater Goggles

6- The Infamous Phone Call

7- How to Make Money in Real Estate at Any Age

8- Adapting and Changing in Different Situations/Survival

**Cover Art Created by Quinton Prunty**

My goal for this book is to inspire motivated young people to start a business and not be afraid to do whatever you want.

I want you to not be scared about the world and do whatever you feel is your destiny.

Writing this book and putting in all the long nights, long days and over 100 hours was amazing. It was an experience unlike any other and I hope that at least one person gets up and takes a shot at their dream.

I poured my heart and soul into his book, and everything I believe is in this book.

Please enjoy and reach out to me after you read it. I would love to hear all opinions.

"The $8,000 Phone Call"

**Chapter One**

**The Beginning**

**How I first got started in business/self-employment.**

"The more people you meet, the more you'll eat." -Gallant Dill

I first got started in business back in elementary school. I was around 9 or10 years old in the 4th and 5th grade. I didn't always have enough money for lunch every day and my mom was selling bracelets and necklaces on eBay and PayPal. She was only selling them for like fifty cents to a dollar apiece but most of it was profit. She asked me to sell some of these at school and of course I said yes.

    The first couple of days were slow because nobody my age had money but I told the kids to ask their parents for money. I was hustling all day at school and lunch trying to sell them. I believe that in a couple of days I sold five bracelets all at once and made enough money to buy pizza at lunch and I was so PUMPED. I made about four or five bucks in the second day of selling and hustling.

    My mom expanded her inventory slightly and we started selling on the side of the road at an area where everybody sold whatever they had. People gathered every weekend on this corner of the street to sell all kinds of items like a community yard sale. But of course, eventually the city decided to shut it down since they (the city) weren't getting paid. They always need to take away anything that doesn't benefit them. Sound like somebody else? "Government."

    So, we moved to online markets like eBay and Amazon. We sold quite a few more of the bracelets and necklaces then we launched new products like lanyards, keychains, etc. It was fun and I enjoyed being able to eat pizza at lunch and my mom had some extra spending money as well which she loved. Eventually we stopped making/selling the products. I learned some valuable lessons during that time. It taught me that if you have a product that people want, you can control the market and make profits. Businesses come and go, only the strong and stable ones, like Coca Cola and Walmart continue to thrive. To succeed and keep your business operating for the future, you must innovate and adapt with the people/market.

My product died as kids got older and I didn't adapt with what people wanted. My bad of course. Those were invaluable lessons at this young age.

That's when I think I first got bit by the "business bug". Now I just buy and sell products on eBay along with my primary businesses. You can always come back to an old business. There's no rush on success! The only time you can be considered a failure is when you completely abandon the idea and stop working towards it. That's when you have failed. But let's fast forward about 5-6 years to when I can legally get a job in Arizona.

Since I had developed a taste for business and money, I wanted as many jobs I could after with school. (School stops you from doing a lot). As a school kid I wanted as much money as possible and it felt good doing something that I knew no other kid was doing. Also, my parents didn't buy me anything special unless it was a holiday (which is a key in why I'm successful) it's all about how you are raised. You are a seed and your parents must nurture you in a certain way otherwise you grow spoiled and become a victim in the world.

The first job I ever worked was with my dad doing construction. I basically just helped carrying lumber, strictly manual labor. It was an amazing job paying $10 an hour, a boon for a fifteen-year old. That's more than most middle aged people get now. It was awesome, barely working 10 hours a week and making $100 weekly. Though that was way more than I needed I wanted more. It's not about making money, it's about growing as an individual and becoming independent. I liked buying my own necessities. like books, electronics and a reliable vehicle. Those are key when growing up. Always invest in yourself, trust me it's worth it. So, I worked with my dad during the summer school vacation for 2-3 years.

During school I needed something to do and somewhere to work. I looked all over for a job and asked everybody I knew if they knew of a good place to work was because I didn't want any fast food job. I wanted something I could move up in or have the potential to make more money. It's hard finding a job like that at 15 years old and having almost zero experience.

The only thing I knew I could do was handle people and count money fairly quickly. My aunt and mom recommended I get a job at the Renaissance festival in Gold Canyon. My Aunt Elaine had worked there when she was younger and said that she could make tips and it was pretty fun. It was only a few weeks before it opened and most jobs were already filled except one bakery job at this little Mom & Pop shop. They needed somebody to help out around the shop and clean up and of course I said yes! It was like $8 per hour, all cash under the table. Shhhh. Don't tell anyone. I worked about 9-10 hours per day on the weekend and cleared about 160 bucks a weekend. Again, not bad for a weekend job that didn't affect my school work. I simply had to sacrifice my weekends for money, which many people my age weren't willing to do. But I was and that's what made me different. You'd be surprised how many people are lazy and unwilling to put any effort forward unless they get Immediate results. So, if you can just give it 100% of your effort and put all attention to it, you will become successful. Once you give it everything you have and put in the time, you are in the 5% of people who are doing the same thing. You're not fighting against everybody to become successful, only the small handful of people who are giving it their all to make it before you. You aren't going against 100% of the population, only 5%. The other 95% aren't even in your league ambition wise or will work as hard as you.

    Stay committed and stay focused. If you can break big things down into little tasks and little goals, you will accomplish everything you need to do. Whatever you do, know that you need to learn it and master it. It's a crazy concept to go out and do whatever it takes to become successful. It's so crazy that few people do it. When people ask me, "Jayden, what should I do? How do I do this? Nobody's going to hire me."

    They cry and complain about everything. I say, "Okay, so what have you tried?"

    They mention something that they tried that had very little impact because it wasn't big enough then they make more excuses of why they haven't done more. When you try to confront them as to what they did and for how long, they will say, "I don't know."

    If you don't, a rough estimate of how long you did something or when you did it, it wasn't important enough to you. If you want to be successful, hang around successful people, if you want to be a mechanic, hang around mechanics and tools. Whatever you want or want to be, surround yourself with it, make it all you think about every single day and I promise you, you will get whatever you're working for. It's such an easy thing to do but must people won't do it because they can't afford it or don't want to waste time because it's not a guaranteed success. Nothing is guaranteed! You must go out and want to make it happen. Nothing in this world is guaranteed to you. You need to go out and seek it for yourself. If you want to make things happen you have to get uncomfortable and go hustle. Period. If you want the nice cars and big houses work as hard as you can every day, then go look at the houses you can't afford and sit in the cars you can't drive yet. Visualize that you are living where you want to live and doing things you want to do for the rest of your life and you are already halfway there.

I started cleaning cars in my spare time between jobs and school. This was really my first self-employed kind of gig. I never did anything before this without somebody telling me what to do and how to do it. I really enjoyed cleaning/detailing cars because I liked having a clean truck and making dirty vehicles spotless. I did that on and off for myself and family for about two years until I realized I turned 16 and took it official and worked at a car wash to detail cars for money.

After I got more experience detailing as a job, I decided to start detailing for myself as a side business because I knew I could make a lot more money. That's when I knew I was destined to make money being self-employed and I could get out of the 9-5 life. I believe the dream for everybody is to just be happy doing what they love and getting paid for it. The beauty behind doing what you enjoy and what you love, is that even when you struggle and go through hardships, you'll still be smiling because you are happy and so the money will follow. The number one thing people ask you when you get a new job or have an idea for a career is, "how much money do you make?" Why is that? Nobody will ever ask you if you are happy doing it or how happy this job will make you. All most people care about is the money. One major way you can tell how mature and advanced as a thinker a person is, is by the questions they ask you whenever you are around. Why do you think an employer at a new job asks you, "do you have any questions for me?" It's because they want to see how advanced of a thinker you are and how intelligent you are.

Always ask a question when they ask! They want to know if you were paying attention because there is always something you can ask. Don't be afraid to speak up and show them who you are. When I started working harder and people began realizing that what I was doing was succeeding, everybody asked me how much money I made and if they could do it, too. I would always respond, "but you don't even know what I do, why would you want to do it?" I could sell human body parts and make all that money, it didn't matter, people just want the money to be happy.

Of course, being an entrepreneur isn't just a job that you fill out an application for and apply. It's a lifestyle that you dedicate your entire life to. It's not from 9 a.m. to 5 p.m. An entrepreneur "job" is 24/7, from when you wake up until you go to bed. Even then I dream about growing and things I could better. A real way to determine if somebody is ready to be an entrepreneur or business owner is asking them, "are you willing to work 60-70+ hours per week?" Many will say, "of course not, I have this and this and this." Blah blah blah, they will hit you with a million and one excuses. Just tell them, "you're not ready to be an entrepreneur yet." Some days you will work 10+ hours for not a dime, while on others you will work a few hours for a couple hundred dollars.

You will not make money every day being an entrepreneur, especially starting out. You might go days, weeks and even months without seeing a single dollar bill. I went 12 months without seeing a single check from real estate. Most people aren't willing to do that. That's okay, that's where the real hustlers and the real go getters come in and become successful. I firmly believe people will do anything for a large enough amount of money. But once people get enough money to support themselves and they no longer need to work as hard for the money, they will soon realize that they are unhappy and picked something they hate just for the money. I know so many people that picked a career solely based on the "estimated income". Then once they get into doing it, they don't make the money they expected and they become unhappy and are forced to reset all over again. I'm not saying that you should pick one idea and go for it and don't ever change. I am saying take some time to figure out what really makes you happy and what you enjoy doing. Whatever you love doing right now, make that your job for the rest of your life. The longer you take to calculate and plan your life job, the better chance you have of never changing "jobs" ever again. If I have one piece of advice to give anyone at my age it would be this, the job you're working now, will not be the only job you will ever work. This is not the peak of your life, just because you're young doesn't mean that you have to be the best at this age; starting as early as possible ensures that you pass everybody on the way and become successful before everybody around you. It's really scary to start out your life, and then go against what everybody taught you growing up and go with your gut. Most won't do it because they were taught to live the 9-5 and pay bills and die. Most people go through life thinking this and following this until they get old and wonder why they lived a terrible, unfulfilling life. Just do whatever you want to do and don't let anybody tell you differently. People are going to judge you anyway, so you might as well do whatever you want to do.

    When I started to grow personally by increasing my jobs I worked and businesses I started, I began to change/grow as a person. For the better, of course. I think it's crazy when people say "success changed you." Of course success changes people, the goal wasn't to stay the same. Success will ALWAYS change you in some way or form. It will change the way you think, speak and act. Friends and family will always support you when you start your journey knowing that you probably won't achieve the goal or accomplish anything. (Messed up, right?) They support you fully as a type of pity, like they feel obligated to support you until you start doing better than them. Chances are when you start your success journey most of your family will be better off than you because they are older and have much more experience, but trust me age has nothing to do with anything. The moment you start showing them that you have a chance of succeeding or start growing, their view about you will change. Most of the time they will make a bunch of excuses for why you're doing so well and they are not. They will say it's because they are too old or had kids too early or some other stupid excuse. They will tend to say that the world is against them and that it's too late for them. These people are called "victims". Victims of the world's actions and consequences. These people can be the closest family or friend but when you head down this success journey, your eyes will open and you will see "victims" very clearly.

Most of these types of people wait for the "perfect" time to start doing what they always wanted to do. Most people wait their whole life to start that business or make the leap. Yes, it's riskier as an adult to make the jump because you may have kids, bills and other things the "victims" are scared to lose. That's why it's much easier to make the jump as a kid or young teen because you have so little to lose and so very much to earn. You just cannot be afraid of fear and failure, they must be your best friends. Fear and failure will grow you into the person you've always wanted to become -- I guarantee it. Concentrate on the things that make you uncomfortable but move you forward, don't waste your time on anything that doesn't grow you or earn you income. You have to train your mind to push aside things that don't grow you or make you money. As you advance in your business life, you will need to map out your day doing only the things that are vitally important to you and your business. If you have time at the end of the day you can do some silly things but you must get everything done that needs to be done. Because if you don't, you will push it aside and procrastinate which is a nasty habit that you never want to adapt. A good way to get big things done every day is to do the thing that's the hardest or most uncomfortable at the beginning of your day. So, jog that mile in the morning or write that paper when you wake up. Now, the rest of your day is much easier and you can enjoy your day far more. It's the relief of stress being lifted off your shoulders, you feel much happier during the day and just your overall mood is lifted. Either way, you have to stay on your path and keep moving forward. Never backwards. You will find things that will keep you motivated and working hard day after day. That's important, since you will not always feel the same way every day since you are just starting out and not having much success.

I know Tai Lopez does something that keeps him working hard every day. One of his tips is, work hard all day long and hang out at night with your friends and go eat or see a movie. Always have something to look forward to every day so you stay motivated and working hard. When you have a prize to get every day and you work all day, it makes you enjoy that reward even more. It's a feeling like no other to work hard and say, "Wow, I deserve this!" I really hate when people go out and party almost every weekend just to celebrate nothing. Just because it's the weekend doesn't mean you need to celebrate it...when the reality is you're broke and can barely afford the rent this month. I will never understand how people can spend every dime they have just to party and get messed up. I never partied in high school and don't regret it. I had way bigger things on my mind and it's paid off in major dividends in my life after school.

Many people that partied every night and wasted their precious high school years come to me and ask me how I do it. They ask, "How did you just get successful and make that money?" Nobody knew all the late nights I spent up working on my business and figuring out how to close my first deal. I stressed my whole senior year and spent so many nights awake thinking about my future and how I could create it. The only way those people will ever know how hard I worked and why I did is through this book. Only a few people knew what I was doing during school. Everybody used to judge me for all the things I did. They used to laugh and think I was an outcast, a loser, every name you can imagine for not partying on the weekend.

Well, who's laughing and doing better now? That's right, me. All those kids who laughed at me and just wasted their weekend away, now ask me for money and guidance! They come to me for advice, having no clue what they should do with their life. Being the person I am, I do help them. I give them small tips but nothing major. If they really want me to help them, I charge per hour. They say, "Why should I pay you or why are you charging me, BRO?" I say, "I'm charging you because you wasted all your time drinking, smoking and partying while I used my time wisely to be in the position I am in today. I'm charging you for all the long nights I stayed up studying and working towards my dream that you now want me to share with you and teach you. That's why. BRO."

You can start a business from any niche, by which I mean something you specialize in or something you do better than anything else you do. Or something you are the best at doing. It could be art, speaking to people, selling product, fixing cars, etc. You can start a business out of anything nowadays. Social media is getting huge and blowing up. Because back in the old days starting a business required labor or some sort of skill but now you can start a business creating YouTube videos or editing photos. Anything you do better than anybody else, you can turn into a business. It may seem easy but it might not be. Most people think you can just start a business and run it, which is partly true but it's not as easy to maintain that business and continue to grow it. Yes, your business must grow and get better, or people will get better than you and destroy you. Business is a dog eat dog world and you have to constantly be growing and becoming the best in the market. That's because there's always somebody out there willing to be better and work harder if you're not. I believe that you always have to be innovating and becoming better every day or growing in some way. I've see people run their business the exact same way for 5, 10, 15+ years. If we have changed the vehicles we drive, the phone we use and the food we eat, doesn't that mean people have changed too?

Seeing these people run their business the same way hurts me. I don't think I'm anywhere close to knowing how everything works in their particular business, but what I do know is how to change and innovate your business for the better. I know how to change what you're doing currently and make it better. There's always a better way to do everything rather than just sticking with the status quo. That's how new inventions thrive. People will always pay to do something easier and faster. That's why we make faster cars, self-driving cars, Amazon fresh food service. You name it, the sky's the limit.

I'll say this, if you have found an easier or faster way to do something and it makes sense, take that business idea and run with it. Put everything you have into it. Because I know that anything that makes people's lives easier, will be successful. I dare you to go and look at some businesses that are failing and figure out why. It's a fun game and usually it's quickly apparent to any business person with their eyes open. The problem with old mom and pop businesses is that they are stuck in the old ways of business, they aren't current with marketing online, Facebook and websites. They think if their method worked before it will continue to work. Now, don't get me wrong. You don't have to change your business entirely just to grow, but you do have to tweak what you're doing to appeal to the current generation.

If there is something you think would be a great business like opening a supplement store or a smoothie shop for example, I want you to go to all the stores in your area and jot down your observations of the pros and cons on that business. Write down what they lack and things you think you could do better than them. Because if you can start your business with all these great ideas and great ways to be better than the other stores in your market, you will be successful. You have to be extremely dedicated to your idea, because if you don't believe in what you do, who else will? You have eat, sleep and breathe your business. It doesn't matter how big the companies are or how much you think you couldn't compete with such a big name because you're so small. It literally doesn't matter. If you know you can be better and prove it, you will indeed be better and sure enough you will beat the competitor. If you haven't quit your day job yet while you're trying to open this business, take small steps every week that will add up at the end of the month into big bold moves. People think you can start a business and know exactly how to operate it in a couple of days or a week. That's not true. You just have to break down everything you need to start the business and get the ball rolling. Every week set new goals for yourself that progressively develops your business. Always do at least something every week and never fall backwards or stop.

  Everybody has time to do anything they want. Even if you work a 9-5 job you can come home and work at least 1-2 hours on your business if you really want it badly enough. Or in the morning before work, wake up early and work on that business. If you are sneaky enough and depending on your job, you can sneakily work on your business at work! People always make the excuse, "I don't have enough time" but these people are just uninspired and unmotivated. If you have a clear vision and you work hard towards whatever you wanna do, you will make that time and become successful. The sooner you start and the faster you can get the ball rolling, the sooner you can quit your 9-5 job and focus just on your business. The best feeling in the world is working for yourself and being able to control your income and not have anybody tell you what to do to earn that money. Since I was 18 years old I have been unemployed and had no job whatsoever. I started my journey by just jumping in without any safety net to support me or anything to fall back on. I just thought "swim or die". I had no other choice because I was tired of working for other people. And believe me it was the greatest thing I've ever done and I don't regret any of it.

Once you become successful and you look back at yourself and when you first started out, you will laugh. You will think, *what was I even worried about.* I would much rather look back and laugh at being scared in the past, than living with the regret of not starting that business or think what could've been. I think that is the worst thing that could happen, living with regret and being too afraid to have ever even given it your best shot. Fear can hold you back and freeze you from doing something you know you could do. They say money isn't everything. That's true, but living with debt and being broke isn't much either. Don't ever do anything just for the money. Do it because you're passionate about it and you wanna do it. I promise that money will follow whatever you do that you are very, very passionate about. If you currently work a job and make okay money doing it, don't be afraid to invest. People always come to me and say, "Jayden, I have $500, what should I do with it to make more money?"

I always reply, "$500 isn't enough for anything except investing in yourself, take that whole $500 and buy books, audio books, knowledge, online courses, something that applies to what you wanna do."

Then they say, "I don't really read books or have time to sit time and listen to study an online course."

Well, if you don't read books, you aren't ready to be successful or ready to grow into the new you if you aren't willing to invest If you won't invest $500 in yourself, why would anybody else pay you money? People don't pay you because you're cute or strong, they pay you because they believe in you that you can get the job done. They are investing that money into you so you will get the job done.

Most people struggle so hard to have the courage to spend money on a book or other tools that will help grow you as a person but have no problem spending money at the club or at the movies. I never understood how people could complain about their job and money when they have no problem going out with friends to spend whatever money they have. That right there is people settling for temporary fulfillment over long-run accomplishment. If you want to start a business or be an entrepreneur, you need to cut out all that extra spending and time you spend with friends. Be ready to give up those weekends with friends and spending every night eating out. Get ready to start spending money on yourself and writing checks to grow yourself. You might spend money on things that aren't even physical. It could be online data and books. Creating a business is very easy, anybody can do it, but transforming yourself into that successful mindset person, the NEW you...*that* is very hard and that is when most people give up. It's extremely difficult. You've spent your whole life acting and thinking the same, but now you have to change the way you do everything and the people you talk to. It takes a lot from yourself but the rewards are amazing and it's worth every hard minute you went through.

But most people will never get to experience the fruits earned from struggling and working so hard towards a goal. People are just fine with living a 9-5 life wondering why they feel so empty and unfulfilled. People will burn the wood for the bridge for temporary warmth rather than build the bridge to get where unlimited warmth is abundant. If it doesn't benefit people right away, most will turn away and won't do it. The majority mindset of people is that if doesn't work right away, it won't ever work.

## Chapter Two

### Starting A Business While in High School

"Formal Education will make you a living; Self education will make you a fortune."-Jim Rohn

This chapter will be about how I juggled real estate while still in high school and managed to get good grades. I'll talk about how I managed to close my first deal while still in school by taking calls between classes and setting appointments when I stepped out of class. I was very different from everybody else with a different mindset and different goals. It's okay to be different when you know exactly what you want. Everybody doubted me but towards the end of my senior year everybody wanted to know how I did it. I wasn't a straight A student for sure because I was distracted by making an income in real estate and becoming successful. I was distracted by doing something with my life and I knew high school wasn't going to teach me the things I needed to know and to go where I wanted to go. College wasn't going to take me where I needed to go to become successful either, that's why I didn't really pay that much attention to my classes the last two years of high school. I would also post Craigslist deals during class and call leads during lunch. It was a struggle trying to operate a business while in high school! I attended Apache Junction High School in Apache Junction, Arizona from age 14 to 18. Yeah, it wasn't the nicest school for sure or had the best teachers. I feel the school system was super corrupt and everybody pulls money from the system more and more every year. Towards the end of high school around my junior and senior year, the school literally had zero dollars in the bank to pay for anything. So, they pulled the money from the students in order to keep the school afloat. The school charged more and more per student per year as much as they could in little amounts so nobody would notice. Little things like charging 50 cents more for lunch, vending machine expenses went up and parking passes increased. When anything in price increases, the product should be upgraded, if it doesn't, the business is getting greedy for no reason. At least they could change it up in some way. The lunch was the same nasty mess, the vending machines were still broken, old and nasty and the parking lot still needed plenty of repairs like lights and roadway maintenance. It was a MESS!

    Everybody said we were the first to get all new laptops to carry around and take home but what you do not know about is all the fees and policies that followed those stupid laptops. They charged insurance for all the laptops and any type of normal wear and tear done to the computer was counted against you and the students paid for it. One of my close friends, Trevor, had about $300-$400 in computer damages! The school didn't start out that way. They didn't used to charge all the students for little damages. But either way I hated these things because you always have to worry about not breaking them, dropping them or harming them in anyway. I couldn't even use them to my advantage for business because everything was blocked online and they tracked everything I did. But believe me, in class I wasn't doing schoolwork most of the time or studying. Nonetheless, I was leveraging computer technology to my advantage to comp properties and looking up homes in the area I was trying to buy in. I was running numbers and posting Craigslist ads, responding to emails and following up with sellers. I was busting my butt in school my senior year trying to do my first real estate deal. If I could give one piece of advice to anybody in my age group that I learned from all my experiences in high school and growing as an individual, it is this: use every resource you have to your advantage 100%. If you have a resource or an advantage that nobody else has, squeeze every last drop you can out of it. I see way too many people squandering their resources because they think they are unlimited and will have them forever. But in reality, you won't. In most cases, you will have little to nothing with which to work. Use what other people don't have and feed off it! That's one very major way to become successful.

You can easily start a business in any environment and at any age. Age does not define you. The number one excuse I hear from people is, "I'm too young" or "I'm too old" to become successful. I hate hearing this, it drives me nuts and gives me goosebumps every time I hear it. Why? Because it's so not true. There are many examples to prove this notion is incorrect. I can give you names of a bunch of people who were super old when they become successful and kids who became successful. But instead I'll just give you two good examples of people who were very young and very old and still became successful. The first person I'll talk about is Caleb Maddix. This kid is 14 years old! Only 14 years old! He is one incredible person and I will have the pleasure of meeting with him after this book is published. He has accomplished many things already and such a young age. He is a self-published author of the book *Keys to Success for Kids* selling more than 100,000 copies. He is also a public speaker and a true American entrepreneur. This kid has what many people don't. Heart. He's a daily motivational speaker with over 2 million views on YouTube. He also offers a daily one on one life coach program for an entire year when you sign up for his "kids 4 success" program. I thought I was doing well and was far ahead being only 19 years old until I saw what this kid has done with his life already as a fourteen year old adolescent. This just goes to show that no matter what you are doing, no matter how well or how bad you think you have it, there's always somebody doing better or worse than you. You are never at the very bottom where nobody has had a harder life than you and there's nobody that has ever done the best of everything. He has very big plans for the rest of his life and what he is to become. He expressed that as far as money goes, he wants to be a millionaire by sixteen and a billionaire at 30. He doesn't care about the money though, he cares about the people he impacts. He wants to speak to 100,000 people under one roof and do a TED talk. Caleb even said his biggest goal is to be able to give a large check to single mothers with kids and help them succeed and just survive. Caleb doesn't care about how many people go to his funeral, he just cares about how many people cry because those are the people he impacted on a personal level and those are the people who really matter to him.

So, what does that tell you about this kid? Does he have more than 24 hours in a day? Does he have some super human power that enables him to get more done in a day? Or does this kid just cheat his way through? People will make up all kinds of excuses for why he is so successful and why they aren't. They will say, "Oh well, he had help to become successful," or, "He was rich growing up so it was easy for him to become a speaker." None of these are true! He came up from being super poor with his dad by his side but he knew exactly what he wanted in life where he wanted to go and how he was to get there. He worked harder than anybody his age and he became successful because he wanted it so badly! Caleb didn't just sit around and play video games, watch Netflix and sit on his butt all day. He put the work in and the hours to make it happen. So why haven't you become successful at 30, 40, 50+ years old? Maddix is 14 years old and has done all these things that most people only dream about! That's just one example of a person who was too "young" to become successful *but he was.* Many people nowadays think they need to wait for the perfect moment or a signal to bring their idea to life. If you are one of those people, stop it now, if you wait for the "perfect" moment, you will be waiting forever, I promise you that. You won't hit the lottery and create that business. Most people who win the lottery are selfish and do not deserve all that money. No matter what anybody says money will change who you are as a person. Whether it changes you for the worse or the better is up to you but ultimately it will change you in some ways. People who live paycheck to paycheck making $300, $400 a week then suddenly come into millions of dollars are in a bad situation. Many of us have no idea what to do with all that money as far as investing and making more money with it and they just end up spending it on stupid stuff like cars and houses that they can afford. That's why business owners who come into big money like that know how to use the money and spend it wisely and put it into investments.

    Mainly older people win the lottery over anybody really but there's another older person I wanna talk about who didn't win the lottery but instead worked hard to build his empire. He was a failure his whole life and only become successful when he was in his mid-60s. Most people don't even know the story behind this man even though he is a real example of age does not matter. Most of you drive by one of his many restaurants around the country and pay little attention to it. I bet most of you even go there to eat and don't even know who created it. Well, the person I'm about to talk about did not become successful until he was 65 years old, living on Social Security and retired. How's that for being old and dried up? Wouldn't you think once you got to that age you'd be done with everything and just relax? This man had something different in mind. I wanna introduce you to Mr. Colonel Harland Sanders, the creator and owner of Kentucky Fried Chicken. He's the perfect example for anybody thinking they are too old or past the "bar" for becoming successful or creating a business. Sanders is a man who ran a restaurant for several years before entering retirement at the prime age of 65.

When he retired he was broke but not finished. He was determined to share his finger licking chicken with the world because that was one thing for which he was known. Before he created KFC he was making and selling his chicken locally and in his restaurant. So, with little to no money to his name or in his bank account, he traveled by car across the country to different restaurants cooking his chicken in front of the owners. If the owners liked his chicken, they would make a deal and sell it in their restaurant.

Legend has it that he went to 1,009 restaurants before one of them said yes and sold his chicken. How many of you have tried anything more than 10 times let alone 1,009 times? Why didn't he just give up at 100 times of hearing the word no? If I heard the word "no" 500 times I would feel a little discouraged and down. But would you keep going if you heard the word "no" that many times? Can you imagine if he stopped going around at the one thousandth "no" heard? If he stopped at number 1,000 and didn't keep going nine more times, we would have no KFC today and nobody would have ever heard about Colonel Sanders. The initial deal was that for each piece of chicken the place sold, Sanders received a nickel. This was back in the 1960s when a nickel was worth about 0.45 cents in today's money. The restaurant would receive packets of the herbs and spices used to make the chicken so good, without the restaurant ever knowing the recipe. Sanders was smart in doing this because if the restaurant found out the recipe and discovered how to make it, they could easily go around Sanders and push him out of the equation.

By 1964 Sanders had 600 franchises selling his famous chicken and sold his company for two million dollars but remained as the spokesperson. In today's current market, the $2 million is worth approximately $15.6 million. Not too bad for some fried chicken, huh?

By 1976 the Colonel was ranked the world's second most recognizable celebrity. So, next time your grandpa or grandma has an idea for a business or thinks they could make something that everybody could use, tell them to go for it!

Another famous entrepreneur that I'm sure all of you know, is Mr. Grant Cardone. He is a motivational speaker, author, real estate investor and godfather of sales! He owns a real estate portfolio worth $500 million, his net worth is around the same and he continues to grow his portfolio every year. He runs a "young hustler" show every week and has seven published books and wants to write even more! He's referred to as the godfather of sales and sells many programs to help you sell products better and become super rich. Did I mention he's 58 years old and has accomplished all this? He posts motivational content on all his social media platforms. He has influenced so many people and changed so many lives. Grant changes the lives around him on a daily basis. He hires new people every week, gives new opportunities and creates so much content to help everybody become successful and rich. I guarantee he has changed their lives and the futures of the companies he's helped grow and make more money. You can go as far as saying that he changed his kids' lives and the way they are going to grow up. All those families and kids to come will all remember Mr. Grant Cardone. He launched a "mannequin challenge" on YouTube and 955,000 people viewed it within one day. In just one day he reached out to just about a million people and that was just because of a silly office video challenge. Imagine how he changes the people who view the videos he posts about being successful and his Young Hustler show.

Ever since I started following Cardone's social media and watching his videos I feel more confident doing the job I do and a better job selling. His free videos and books have changed the way I think and do business, it opens a different alleyway of thinking that you most likely didn't have before. Just in the past couple months of reading his 10x book and the millionaire booklet, it changed me. I couldn't imagine how he changed people's entire lives over the past ten years. But he didn't become successful and own this huge real estate portfolio until not too long ago. He was a bad kid growing up. Grant said that he did all the stupid things like drink, smoke and just about every other stupid thing that didn't benefit his well-being. Everything you do every day should grow your or benefit you in some way. It wasn't till he was older that he realized he needed to get his life together and make something of himself and moved from accounting with no money and went into automobile sales. What if he just decided to give up and worked a 9-5 job the rest of his life because he didn't recognize his own potential? He wouldn't have gone into automotive sales and become the godfather of sales, and he wouldn't have created the massive real estate portfolio he has now. It would have been very easy for Grant to give up and say, "I'm too old for this shit." His excuse would have been, "Well, I'm too old to become successful" but look at him now. Doing the best that he's ever done and will continue to do even better. Now Forbes rates him #1 of "25 marketing influencers to watch in 2017". I bet he never thought he'd ever be here 10-15 years ago!

That's just one of the sad things about small-minded people, they think if they encounter any challenge, it's not for them. These people think the path is going to be perfect and they won't run into any problems or struggle. Working a 9-5 you will rarely run into problems but you will run into being BROKE. Being small-minded and not willing to struggle will hold you back from accomplishing so many things in your life. I'm sure glad Grant Cardone didn't give up and quit when he got older because many people would never be the same. I guarantee so many things have not been invented yet because somebody thought they were too old and couldn't do it.

This is a very sorry excuse not to start a business or create wealth. These victims of society need to come up with better excuses because this is a very bad one. Please never come to me and give me the excuse about your age again, I'm done with it. After you read this chapter, quit making all the excuses, take responsibility and go get it!

School/college isn't always the perfect and safe path that everybody told you while you were growing up. Especially nowadays in the modern age when a diploma doesn't mean the same as it did ten years ago. Being an entrepreneur seems to be popular and is a word that's very overused. Once anybody becomes unemployed for a few weeks and sells something, they become an entrepreneur. However, that doesn't make you an entrepreneur, it makes you self-employed. Those words are similar but not identical. Being an entrepreneur entails an entirely different lifestyle. Of course being an entrepreneur means you're unemployed, it also means you look at everything that comes your way through new eyes. You view every opportunity that presents itself as an investment and a means to make money.

Being an entrepreneur is a 24/7 365 days a year job. It's not a 9-5 kind of day job, where you wake up and go to a certain location to make money. When you wake up as an entrepreneur your day isn't planned. You could wake up and do something entirely different than what you thought when you woke up. I wake up every day not knowing where I could end up and go that day. Yes, you should have some sort of daily planner every day or plans every week but you should be willing to do something you didn't think you were going to do. When you are an entrepreneur, you have to be willing to do something new and uncomfortable every day in order to grow. If you think being an entrepreneur is waking up and driving to go pick up a check and then celebrate every night, you aren't even close to the truth and should go get a

9-5.

    This also isn't college or high school. When you get up and get dressed for school every morning you know what most of your day is going to look like. You go to your classes, eat lunch, go home and probably take a nap or watch Netflix. I hate when people know exactly what's going to happen with their day, every day. I never know what I'm going to do on any given day. When people ask me my schedule I say, "I don't know, it depends." Your schedule and daily life should be scrambled and full of improving activities. Your parents and family in general will always tell you to complete high school and go to college. They say get a good job, move into a place and work the rest of your life. What they don't tell you is how to become happy and be fulfilled. Most people's parents grew up being taught the same thing from their parents and now they are miserable feeling empty but still preach the same thing to their own kids hoping something will somehow change along the way. Unless your parents are rich business owners, they won't understand today's modern entrepreneur being self-employed without going to college. Even if your parents are business owners, they probably went to college and got a degree because back when they were growing up they were told they NEEDED a degree. Moreover, even for your parents with a degree, it was a hard for them to start a business, and now you wanna create a business without going to school and teaching yourself? They will literally think you are insane.

    Let me give you a personal example. I have been unemployed and have not received a single dollar from a "boss" since July 9th of 2015. I actually made the jump unaware that I was going to be self-employed. I left my previous job at Men's Warehouse in Mesa, Arizona for two weeks for a vacation to my family farm in Michigan. I quit my job because I knew they wouldn't let me take the two weeks off work and come back. I loved working there but I wasn't going to get promoted to any higher position. I've never worked a job longer than a few months because I always wanted to continuously grow and increase my income and never found a job where I could do that.

    Before I left my old job on vacation I was looking into increasing my self-employed income by detailing more cars while working a 9-5. I was giving myself more time to get ready to quit and work full time on my own. Very scary thing to do at the age of 17/18. This lady came in about a month before I quit officially and was talking about her job at Wells Fargo. We spoke for a little bit and she said they were hiring. Before I left Men's Warehouse, I applied at a couple of Wells Fargo branches near me and left my resumes with all of them. I submitted all of the information before I went on my vacation and was feeling great. So, when I came back from my vacation, I went to a few interviews and waited to get hired. I felt that the job was guaranteed even though I never locked anything up. I was relying so hard on this job because other than my little side business, this was going to be my only income. Even on my vacation I spent most of my money because I thought I was going to get a job and make a great income. I came back and didn't get the job and they wouldn't even tell me why.

    Three months went by and I had almost no money to my name. That's when I discovered real estate and somebody who would change my life forever, Andrew LeBaron. Nothing is guaranteed unless you can hold it or see it with your eyes. Even though my parents and family thought I was crazy for being self-employed at the age of 18, I kept working and pushing hard because I knew I could become successful being an entrepreneur. I knew it would always work out. I knew I didn't want to be told what to do and work for anybody. Once I didn't get that job at Wells Fargo, I made the jump. I was in a swim or drown situation at that point and all I could do was work hard and swim. I made the jump from working at a 9-5 to being self-employed without even knowing I was going to do it. That's a decision that wasn't mine, it was the world's decision. The world basically was telling me to go for it and stop wasting time. The universe was testing me and I'm glad it did. I'm so much better off that I started earlier rather than later.

But the adults of the old generation don't understand that. They worked a job, retired, got Social Security, and then died. That's it. Only a few from the older generation actually made something of themselves. Our parents didn't learn from those people and just listened to their parents before them. "Get a job, create a family and die." That's not how it is anymore, people, we live in such a different world than we did 20-30 years ago, and it's because we are growing. Our parents and indeed most adults in general don't know that you can start businesses out of everything in the 21$^{st}$ century. They don't know about all the millions of dollars teens are making off YouTube and social media marketing. The Baby Boomers just want us to work a job for 50 years, get a check, pay bills and that's it. Well I'm here to tell you that's not how it Is anymore. Life isn't about just making money and paying the bills. It's not about just being able to "get by". Making money nowadays is so much easier than it was back in the Baby Boomers' age. Now our generation just wants to be happy and create a life that's worth living and writing books about. Everybody wants to be self-employed now so we can focus on the more important things in life instead of working. Financial freedom is what we are all chasing now. The ability to be able to go out and do whatever we want with our family and not worry about the check or how much money something is going to cost. One thing I learned from all the experienced and wealthier people I've met is that real bosses pay the check. If you are a real boss, you won't worry about paying the lunch check or expense. You can notice that the person jumping to pay or offering to pay is the guy who feels responsible and has control.

A boss person will jump to pay for anything needed to succeed or a business expense. So, if the opportunity ever arises where you can pay the check, pay it and look like a boss! Take responsibility and it will change your life.

## Chapter Three

## The Struggles/Growth of Your New Self

"I seek opportunity not security."-Les Brown

This chapter is about how you will struggle during the startup and how this phase of your life will shape the person you will become and how strong you really are. The low times will really determine how low you can get and stay determined/motivated, then become successful. The struggle is everything in terms of who you become.

    Being an entrepreneur is a lifelong journey where you grow and evolve every single year. You will never stay steady and remain the same. Never stay idle, always be moving. Most people see all the successful people online but never see the struggling they did. They see everybody driving the brand new Lambo and brand new Ferrari but never see pictures of the old, beat up Toyota pickup that barely ran that these people were previously driving. Because if they posted their old beat up truck and said they are successful and make money, nobody would believe them since they have nothing to show for it. People never care when you talk about starting a business, they only care when you post big, fat checks and brand new cars -- then they ask if you need help. These people will only want to help you when you are already successful and just want to enjoy the lifestyle you have without working for it. People never see the struggle you went through to get all the nice things you have. They will never see the times when you had zero money to your name and nobody wanted to pay attention to you. It's funny, when you are broke and have nothing, everybody pretends to not know you, but when you become successful/wealthy everybody pretends that they are best friends with you. These people are the ones you need to be careful about and stay away from because they will not be loyal to you 100%. They will not be with you when times get tough again and they will fade away.

I know this from experience because I mainly had only one person who stayed with me throughout the struggle and he is my best friend. His name is Donovan. He stayed with me when I struggled through the worst of times up until I got my bigger real estate checks. He didn't care about the money or anything else I had, all he always did was believe in me that I could accomplish anything. He told me we would look back and laugh at our struggle. I always felt bad when he had help me out with money, I hate borrowing money from people. Donovan paid for my food and for my gas a couple of times just so I could drive to real estate appointments. Now Donovan didn't have that much money at the time, he worked at Sonic part time and did pretty good in tips. The crazy thing was that he could barely pay his own bills but he would take care of me first. I'll never forget the times where he had just twenty dollars and he would give it to me. Sit back and think about the people you know who would give you their last twenty. Hard, huh?

There aren't very many people who would do it. Donovan was one of the only people who would do that for me and I'll never forget it. I've had a lot of friends come and go in my life but I know this is one of the few friends I have that will stay for a very long time If not forever down my business journey. I had so many people pretend to be my friend when I started showing signs of becoming successful. They thought if they were my friends during the come up they would get treated well and get money from me. I just ignored these people and you should too. Keep your good friends close and don't ever forget them. Always take care of them and grow together. Always keep testing your friends' loyalty to see how strong it is still. I do it sometimes and I'm always pleased with the results. If you do this and find out all your friends wouldn't put you before a thing, you need new friends. Be careful when you do this because you might end up losing all your friends. This may be a big turning point in your life when you do, so be ready for your whole life to change. Don't be afraid to upgrade friends especially when yours can't keep up with what you are doing and hinder you from growing. Don't ever let your friends slow you down and hold you back. If they are your real friends, they will always keep pushing you and help you grow.

    You will mainly find these great finds during your struggle times. These are the worst of times you will endure and if they want to be friends with you during these times then they will definitely be your best friends that will have your back forever. The only people you should spend your time and energy on are those who were with you during the struggle. You are investing your time, so choose who you spend it on wisely. I only spend my time with the people who I know are going to be successful or those who are already where I want to be and have the things I want. If you want to be successful, hang out with successful people. If you want to own a Lambo, hang out with people that own Lambos already. The law of attraction works so heavily in an entrepreneur it's crazy. Every successful person I know uses the law of attraction by only doing things that push them forward and build them as a person. If it doesn't make you an income or make you better, don't pursue it.

Once you become successful you will only do things that make you more successful. Being a regular/average person you spend your time doing things that make you happy but not necessarily money. Looking back now I realize all the things I could've been doing to better myself rather than the stupid things I was doing. You waste a lot of your life doing stupid things for the instant pleasure, not the long-term fulfillment. Now when I make decisions I think about the future and how this will help me in a couple of weeks, months, years. As an entrepreneur, you always have to be thinking ahead and spend your time wisely on doing different stuff that will help you in the future. You will not always get to enjoy the fruits of your hard work in the beginning but if you work hard enough, the wait will be worth the reward in the end. As an average person, you waste time on TV, video games, relaxing all the time and hanging out with friends all day. All these things aren't bad if you do them in small amounts and not regularly. But the average person doesn't understand this, they want the instant comfort. They don't want to work hard and have to wait for the reward. That's why so many people live the 9-5 lifestyle because they are guaranteed a check every Friday. People get so mad and scared when you hold their paycheck or pay every two weeks. They don't know how to survive during that time and waste their money on stupid things. I feel bad for the people brainwashed into thinking they need to live the 9-5 their whole life. News flash! Fire your boss and start a business. You aren't guaranteed a check every week but once you get good in business, you can make those fat, juicy checks come in every week! Plus, you get to work for yourself and get all the time to enjoy your life. Living the 9-5 your whole life and then complaining about money is the stupidest thing I've ever heard. Of course you're broke and complaining about money, it's because you don't increase your income! You can't have more money without increasing your income some way or another. So, don't be one of those people who just sits there and complains about money, get up and go do something about it. If you really want to be successful and own your own business, you will struggle and fight through it. The struggle determines who is really strong enough to make it and who shouldn't make it.

**My startup and how to manage your money when you have little to zero money coming in week after week.**

I will talk about how to budget every penny you make that you could then pour back into your business and yourself. You will need to pinch every penny and give up a whole bunch of things you were probably used to before, like going out every weekend and eating out. Those days are over until you become GREAT. Not really great, just well off. When you change your income, you change how you buy things and the items you need change. When you open a business/self-employed you stop spending so much money on yourself. Some things I gave up were spending so much time with my friends, going out every day, buying video games and watching TV every single day when I wasn't at work. All those activities didn't benefit my business in any way or benefit me in any way. I stopped doing all that once I became unemployed and working for myself. You, as well, will have to start spending money on your business/self-improvement. Instead of going out every weekend, partying, buying stupid things you don't need and eating out every night, you will have to reinvest all that money back into your business. You can't be so focused on yourself when you are trying to build a successful business. Most likely when you have started to think about/creating your business you have either quit your job or are about to quit. If you are thinking about being self-employed you will need to figure out when you are quitting your job and how. Before you quit you need to try and put yourself in the best possible position so you have an advantage when you do become unemployed. Unless you get fired then you are kind of dead in the water as far as having an advantage. Which is okay too, it's just going to be a little bit harder. Before you quit your job bundle up as much money as possible so you can manage it into your business. You will have to manage every single penny you have stashed already because you will never know when you will see another check or dime again. Kiss making a paycheck every week goodbye and welcome to being an entrepreneur.

When I quit my job and became an entrepreneur I didn't see any big money for about 12 months. It took me almost a year to close my first real estate deal. I went through some very low points during those 12 months where I felt like quitting but then I reminded myself why I was doing what I was doing. I knew I would make it and I knew everything would be okay soon enough. It's very hard to go 12 months without seeing big dollars or even enough to pay for gas. During this time, however, I was making some money doing little side hustles and earning what I could for gas. I was freshly 18 and I had almost no bills to pay, my truck was paid off and I still lived at home of course. I nonetheless felt it was my obligation to pay for myself and make something of my life since I wasn't going to college. I was never one of those kids who felt okay asking their parents for money. I hated asking for money because if I wanted something, I'd work for it and earn it. I never like being handed anything or giving anything to anybody because you are less appreciative. Legends are born in the valley of the struggle. Being handed everything makes you weak and unprepared. If you are handed everything in your life and you never have to struggle, you will be unprepared for when the hard times do come. Then you will be really screwed because you have no idea how to survive during the hard times. I always tell people in my age group that you should start now because you really have nothing to lose at this point in your life. 17, 18, 19 years old you really have no bills, no responsibilities, probably no money to your name and no wife/kids. This point in your life is the best time to bet it all and go for it! You'll never have another opportunity quite like this to make such a life altering jump without risking everything you have. I took the jump at 18 and never looked back.

Of course, there are going to be times when you are so low that you just want to quit and go back to that 9-5 instant money, but you can't. I can promise you whoever is reading this right now, it will be worth the struggle you go through initially. Yourself in 2-3 years will thank you for making that jump now.

Let's say you make the jump and decide to become self-employed and work for yourself. Now what? What should you do the day that you decide that this is it and you're fully committed? The first thing you should do is sit down and figure out what you have financially wise and what exactly you want to do with your life. You need to have all your goals written down and a plan for how you're going to accomplish these goals. That's the very first thing you should do. You can't succeed if you don't know the plan for how to do it. A builder doesn't just build a house with his eyes, he has a blueprint to follow in order to build it right and correctly. Once you have a plan for how you're going to start your business and slowly grow it, then do the math. The number one mistake people make is to assume way too much about pricing and how much something costs. They never know the exact numbers regarding what something is going to cost or what it costs to get to where they need to be. Figure out exactly what it's going to cost to start and run your business.

When you realize how little or how much it's going to cost, that's how you're going to determine how long you need to work every single day towards your business. Yes, being an entrepreneur is a 24/7 job but eventually you won't need to work on your business 24//7 every single day. You will hire other people to run your business while you sit back and profit. But during the beginning you need to set a baseline for your business. Set up a bottom line for what you will accomplish every single day. Set goals for things that you will accomplish every day even when you don't feel it. Like a certain amount of calls you will make, people you will talk to, income per week, etc. This Is a very important thing that most people don't teach you. You won't build your entire business in one day. It just won't happen. So many people overestimate how much they can get done in a day but underestimate what they can do in a lifetime. Nothing great was ever built in one day so why should your business? Take it step by step and day by day. Set small goals for yourself daily and crush them, then whatever you accomplish above that is a successful day that helped to build up your business. Lay the foundation for your business brick by brick so you build a solid business!

Now if you quit your job in order to become self-employed you will have an advantage over the younger people who didn't really have a job/ didn't make a lot of cash before they decided to become an entrepreneur. What you want to do now is assess how much money you have and your expenses every week, such as gas, bills, food, etc. If you are a bit older and just quit your job, you should hopefully have a little money saved up before you quit. Now whatever money you have, you want to keep it close to you and be cautious about what you spend every penny on. Create a graph and figure out how much you'll spend every day, week and month. This way you accurately see how much you need every week. Because you will have to balance your spending and income. Since you're self-employed now, you don't get that check every week!

  You're going to want to pinch every penny you can, that way you are safe for another week of working. If you start running low on funds before you make any money in business there are a bunch of things you can do to earn money. Like ask family members for a loan (pay them back of course), credit cards, and doing side jobs that relate to what you're doing in business. For example, if you are working towards becoming a general contractor, you can work on houses on the weekend for friends and family doing handyman work, and post ads on Craigslist for jobs you know you can do well. Little jobs like that every week will add to more income than you had before. This will hold you off until you start making the big bucks when you get your business going! There's always something you can do as a side hustle that relates to your main business, most of the time you can just Google them! Or get creative.

      During your struggle, you will grow the most as a person both physically and mentally. You won't just become a better thinker but you will live a different life. Everything around you will change and I can guarantee it. You will make everything around you the best it can possibly be if it isn't already. Your body will change as you become healthier and live a better lifestyle. You will change entirely as a person and people will notice, trust me. You will not come out of the struggle the same person you were when you went into it. You will come out better, stronger and wiser! The struggle changes you entirely as a person because it challenges you to think, act and behave differently. I believe the time when you struggle is really the biggest breaking point of your life. It is the biggest thing to happen in your entire life. Legends are born in the hardest of times. It's because the hard times test who you are and test you to see if you are strong enough to succeed. Most people underestimate the struggle but it will be a very big turning point in your life. I went into it head first without even knowing what I was going to expect. I changed the way I view everything after I came out of the struggle and I also became more mature. Before I looked at everything to see if it benefited me and only me. I only cared about myself and I took everything/everyone for granted. If you have any sort of advantage don't take it for granted. Use it as much as you can but always appreciate it every single day and be grateful you have it. I had a vehicle, amazing family and parents who took care of me that I didn't fully appreciate. I took the vehicle that ran for granted, I didn't cherish my loving family the way I should've and I didn't show my parents how much I really appreciated them. When I went through the hard times I realized that they were there for me and supported me the whole time. They helped me out the most they could and I love all my family. Once you come out you will really appreciate everything you have around you and have a new outlook on life.

Everything that comes your way you must use to the fullest extent because you never know when you will get another one. Every opportunity that comes your way you will take and make it the best. A good tip for you would be to look at all the advantages you have right now and be thankful for them. Each and every one of us has some sort of advantage over the next guy. You might not know it but you do. If you sat and actually looked at all the things you can do or skills you have, I guarantee the people around you don't have them. So, use the advantages to their optimum potential.

    I want to give you guys some helpful tips on what to expect as you go into business so you make it through not full of surprises. Tip one, do everything that makes you unconformable. If somebody would've told me that if I do things that make me uncomfortable I'll become successful, things would've gotten better much sooner. I now always challenge myself to do something that I feel uncomfortable about doing but makes me stronger, or talk to at least one new person every day. I do this because I learn something new when I talk to new people in some sort of way. I feel I get along with people and I'm easy to talk to. That's the way a real entrepreneur should be.

Every single person has been down a different path in their life and gone through different things to get to where they are now. I especially love to talk to people who are doing things that I want to be doing. As an entrepreneur, you will always be learning every single day. Like Michelangelo once said, "I am still learning." He said that at the age of 87 because he understood that you will never fully learn anything and there's always something new to learn. No one person knows everything in the world and can't learn something new. Since you are going to be working on yourself so hard mentally, your body will also have to change. You don't see a whole lot of overweight successful people. It just doesn't happen. Why? Because you will be changing so much mentally that your physical body will have to change in order to keep up. You don't have a really fast car that's all dented up and not painted. If you are going to be the best mentally you have to change your body to be the best. During this time in your life is when you will change EVERYTHING about yourself. It's going to happen. Period. Every successful person eventually eats healthy and goes to the gym because they get smarter about what they are doing to their bodies and only want to do the best. They only eat the best foods to give themselves brain fuel and put their bodies in peak condition. If you are producing some of the best content of your life, why would you feed your body junk food? It just doesn't make sense. If you want to be the best, you have to eat and be in the best condition. Don't let your competition take you over. The best way to stay ahead of your competition is to ensure you are the best in every category. And if you can't be the best, work harder than everybody else. When I started doing a little better in business and becoming more successful, I started eating better. Before I even got into business I was already going to the gym and working on myself. I'll tell you this, I've done a lot of deals and made a lot of money at the gym. I have my best ideas here and think the clearest. I don't know what it is but when you work out hard enough either lifting weights or running, you just go into a different mindset. Everything becomes clearer and you think a lot deeper. Some of my greatest ideas have come from being inside the gym. I actually did my first ever real estate deal while at the gym. My advice to everybody would be find somewhere that makes you think clearly and feel comfortable. Somewhere you can think very deep thoughts and brainstorm million dollar ideas. Everybody's got a place where they thought of some million-dollar invention or idea. Find yours and unleash your true best thinking and deepest thoughts. I guarantee once you find this place, you will think of some new ideas. If you're not a good thinker, not talented, not "smart" or any of these things don't worry. You can still be successful in anything you do even if you have zero skills. Want to know how you can still be a successful entrepreneur? Just work hard and it will work out. If you are hungry enough and willing to do whatever it takes, you will become successful. If you are willing to knock on twenty more doors than your competition, you have a lead on him. When he gave up on door number nineteen and you knocked on door twenty, that means you want it more. This will be a part of your success story.

Turn all these struggles of talking to more people, knocking on more doors, calling more people, staying out one more hour than anybody and make them a part of your success story. They say when talent doesn't work, hard work will. You don't need to be talented to succeed, you just need to be hungrier than everybody else. Most likely all your competition has achieved some sort of success and you haven't. Use that as fuel to push you on to the next level! Every day you should wake up with a good attitude and put in the work, because if you don't, somebody else will and it will take you longer and longer. How you look at the roadblocks and push through them will determine what kind of person you will become.

It's not going to be easy waking up every day broke and going to bed broke. It will keep you up at night. I stayed awake many nights trying to figure out how to close deals and make it in this world. The best decision I ever made was to show up and never make excuses and that's what you have to do too! Be willing to take the hits and keep moving forward. Never lower your head, only keep it up and pushing. Life will get easier and easier every day the more hours you put in.

**How to maintain and manage your money when you become wealthier/ start increasing your income.**

Trust me, when you start making some serious bucks, you will have zero guidance on where to spend wisely. Most likely you will spend it on things you don't need which in turn will make you go broke again! Nobody should ever go backwards when you are going so fast forwards. Never slow down and keep your foot on the gas. Sooner or later you will become successful and get big, fat checks. I really hope you become successful sooner rather than later so you can continue to grow, grow and grow even bigger. I hope you get the big checks that change your life. But once you start making consistent money, the $500 check will be just the same as the $100,000 check. The money isn't what matters, it's what you do with it that matters. Starting out, I wanted to just make any amount of money I could consistently. I didn't care if it was $10 a day, as long as I could do it every single day. Once I starting growing, I needed to start growing my income every day. I needed to spend more money in order to make more. I wanted to increase my income tenfold but in order to do that I needed to make more.

See, the thing is, you'll never be happy with any amount of money. I always set a goal for an amount of income but once I get there I always set it higher. In fact, no matter how high I set it, I will always go higher. I will always want more. Because no matter how much you grow or how much money you make, somebody will always be being doing better than you. Yeah, hitting $1 billion a year is cool but people have made way more than that. It will never be enough, so don't chase the money. Chase what you love and the money will just follow. I'm never worried about money because I'm at such a level that I will never go back to broke. I will always come back and make my fortune. That's what you need to chase: knowledge. If somebody would've told me that two years ago, I think I would be in a different place than where I am now. If someone just came from the future and said, "Jayden, don't worry about the money right now, just gain as much knowledge as you can and just learn everything you can," I'd look at life in such a different way and be far more advanced. If anybody ever asked me what the secret to success is, I'd say that the secret is knowledge. I want you to take that tip and go as far as you can with it. I know you will be way better off and I know you will achieve success with just that one tip. If you hate reading books, then you can't be an entrepreneur. You will need to read books and gain knowledge. Period. The reason why this book is entitled "The $8,000 Phone Call" is because when I was just 18 I closed a real estate deal that netted me $8,200 with just a few phone calls and one appointment. Imagine being 18 years old, fresh out of high school and holding $8,200 cash in your hands. I know this isn't anything huge or anything crazy because I know guys my age if not a little older who have done way bigger deals. But seeing a check that big was mind blowing. It took a few days before it even felt real. This wasn't my first deal and it's surely not my last. But right before this deal I was struggling badly because I had invested almost all my money into real estate and into myself. I used all my gas to go to the title agency and pick up this check. I remember not even having enough money to buy two bottles of water at the gas station for me and my best friend Donovan. I went straight to the bank afterward and cashed that bad boy. I had about $7 in my bank account when I deposited some of it and cashed the rest. I just sat back and knew there was no turning back. I knew I couldn't go back to struggling and I had to spend this check very wisely. I couldn't screw it up and go back. I'd reached the point of no return and that was a huge day for me. Mentally, I changed because I still couldn't believe it. It wasn't because of the money, it was the fact that I knew where I was and how far I'd come.

    That next week I just sat back and thought about everything that got me to where I was. I thought about everything in my life and where I was going. It's crazy to think that something that was just a goal/ dream was in my hands and in my bank account. That was the greatest day of my life because of what came after that. The first thing I did with the money was to go out and buy all the supplies I needed for real estate. Paper, printer, software, books, pens, etc. I didn't go out and spend it on watches, clothes or anything that didn't benefit me. Except taking my friends out to eat to celebrate and fill my tank full of gas. I know a lot of people that would take that check and go blow it on parties, cars, expensive clothes, etc. If you ask your closest friends about what they would do with $10,000 right now, I guarantee they wouldn't spend it on things that would better themselves or invest it. The best thing you can do/hardest thing to do is reinvest everything back into your business/yourself. That is the best thing to do when you start getting those big checks. Most people are like deer in the headlights when they see big paychecks, they freeze. I'll be honest when I got my first ever big check I had no idea what to do with it. It was only $3,000 but it was the largest amount of money I'd ever had. I didn't know what to do so it just stayed in my bank account for a while and I barely pulled money for gas. I would say the best thing I could've done is just to pretend I didn't even make the money, pretend I was still struggling and stay as hungry as possible. Getting paid is cool and everything but what you do with that money will determine how far your business will go. The best thing you can do when you get paid is pay off any debts that are small, buy necessary items for your business and continue to work hard. Pretend the money isn't even there because you're so hungry chasing your dream.

I always tell people to work hard and the money will come. Never take a job for the money because whatever you want to do, just do it. Do the things that make you happy and you will never have to worry about money. So, when you do get that check follow a few of these steps and you will be coasting right ahead in your business. Don't let any amount of money interrupt your business. First take that money and put it right in your bank account savings or a business account if you have one. Put 50% of the check away and use the rest of it to survive. So, if you just made $2,000, pretend you only have $1,000 of it to use. Yes, at first it will suck because it's way less than what you want to spend but this will help you in the long run. Use that 50% and buy basic things you need for your business and items you need to go out every day and hustle. Like gas, food and basic supplies. That 50% will sit in your account until you really need to spend it on some big business decision/investment. Grant Cardone talked about this a lot when he started to become more successful. He said, "I was making more money than I've ever made in my entire life but I was still broke." He always put 50% of everything he earned into an account that he could never touch unless he was ready to buy something big for business. You may start making big checks but you will have to learn to put half of everything away. You will seem poor and struggling to most people but what they don't know is the huge amount of money that will be in your account.

You will need to make the most out of your half paychecks and make them work. After a while you will get a system going every time you get paid and it will become easier. Keep hustling like you are still struggling and keep working hard. The only way you can make the half paychecks seem better is by making more of them. By the time you have 2, 3, 4 or even 5 checks coming in every few weeks you won't even notice that half of it is going into a separate account because there will be so many zeros at the end. This is the fastest and most effective way to become wealthy. I use this in my life every week and it's a system that is tried and tested. If you want to be setup in a great position for the future, do this when you make any of sort of money. Trust me, this is the best thing you can do for yourself.

## Chapter Four

### The First Deal; Success at Last

"Successful people are 100% convinced that they are masters of their own destiny, they're not creatures of circumstance, they create circumstance, if the circumstances around them suck, they change them." Jordan Belfort

Building a relationship with the buyer will create much more wealth for you in the future, and relationships are everything in this business when it comes to creating massive wealth. Relationships will mean a lot more down the road in your real estate life. They will help you continue to do more and more deals. Not just in real estate but in any business, creating a relationship with everybody around you will make all your efforts run smoother. Look at all the people who help make your business work and operate. If you build better relationships with those people, it will assure more trust and loyalty between you and them. It also assures these people they are working for somebody who is worth working for and at the end of the day, they will feel a close connection with you. This ensures that everybody has the same mindset and is working towards the same goal.

When you first start any business, foremost on your mind is always the money but as you get more involved you realize that it's not all about the money, it's about the lives of the people you change around you. I will admit that when I first started all I wanted was to be successful and make all the money, but once I began growing as an individual I realized that it's not all just about the money and material wealth. It's about changing your life and the lives of those around you for the better. Once I realized that I started to act differently towards deals and towards money in general. Of course, money is the goal but now that's not always on my mind throughout the deal, what's on my mind is building relationships with the people who are involved with me. I always want to be producing a positive energy and just positive vibes in general towards those people. They always say to treat somebody how you would like to be treated but I say you should treat customers *better* than how you would want to be treated. Always be willing to go that extra mile or do that extra thing to close a deal and make somebody happy. Because at the end of the day we really are not in the business for money, we are in the business of people and meeting new people every single day. You will not succeed If all you can think about is the money.

Change your focus from just money to people and creating solutions. Once you create solutions to people's problems, you will have money flowing in no problem. It's crazy, you think when you focus so heavily on something you want, it will just come in. But that's not always the case. Sometimes when you focus so hard on something, you get tunnel vision and don't work on other things that you need to grow or expand your business. In any business, you must be willing to keep your options open and to do all kinds things to make it work. You mustn't stick to just one certain way to run your business or market. Stay open to doing different things and working in different ways to achieve the goal. I think if you keep an open mind, you can do anything in this world and achieve everything you want. Don't be that person who doesn't or won't try new things when the old ways don't work. Be willing to adapt or you will die.

I'm also going to talk about what it takes mentally to make it through real estate and to close your first deal and to keep closing deals time and time again. Closing deals is literally all mental and acting. You need to have a certain mentality to keep doing deals. Being an entrepreneur is a 24/7 deal. You must get out of the 9-5 mindset and get into the entrepreneur mindset especially if you are going from a job to being self-employed. It takes a lot from you mentally and physically to make that change from a job to unemployed. Most people don't understand that because they were raised to go to school, then go to college and hopefully work a 9-5 job then live off Social Security till they die. And hopefully get a family and a house during the meantime and die somewhat happy. But they will die like they never existed and never leave a mark on the world by leading the basic slave life. That's what it basically is, a slave life! Do this and do that then die. Nothing fun or exciting unless you get a decent house or maybe buy a cool car off retirement money. It's a boring life where you are born and work till you die. Can you convince me to live that life? Heck no you can't. But what you can convince me to do is live life as an entrepreneur. Where you build a company around what you love doing, have unlimited income possibilities and do everything you've ever wanted to do like travel around the world, or buy any car you want and live wherever you want. You basically have the freedom to do whatever you'd like to do and there's no limits when you are an entrepreneur. You get to live the dream you want and the life you see in the movies. There's no 9 to 5 job or a boss yelling at you telling you what to do and when you can have a vacation. When you're an entrepreneur you work when you want while doing what you love and build an amazing team around your business model. You can also take a vacation whenever you like or maybe take a day off or two. Amazing thing is you can do whatever you want versus a 9 to 5 where you must ask to do something that you'd like. You should never have to ask, "Can I take a vacation?" or "Can I hang out with my family? You should build an amazing life that you can do that whenever you want.

But it's crazy. Most people will still argue that working a 9 to 5 and living securely every week is the best way to live. They will say, "Well, it's hard to think of something and create a business around it" or, "Well, you don't get paid every week and nothing is certain." These are all very lame excuses not to go out and get what's yours and what you deserve and what your family deserves. The only hard part about being an entrepreneur is in the beginning when you're starting everything up. But you're setting yourself up in building a life that you want to live forever. Once you start creating that business then produce income then monetize it to run 24/7 without you even there, it's game over and you can live your life however you want. Of course, it's going to be hard at the beginning. Everything that's worthwhile takes time and effort. Nothing that's meant to last is easy to come by. The harder the road the greater the reward is what I've always preached. The more you work now and the harder it is, the easier it will become and the bigger the reward you shall receive. But living an amazing life and doing whatever you want is not for everybody.

I know some people that just can't get their mindset to switch from being a slave 9-5 to owning their own business and working for themselves. But hey, that's them. You won't be able to convince everybody about the life they could live if they worked hard every day and hustled. These are the people you should try to help a few times then kind of forget. You don't need to waste your time with these people.

Move on and only focus your time on those with the same mindset as you. Like I said before, wasting your time is worse than wasting money because you can always make more money but not more time. That's why you should invest your time and energy into people and ideas that deserve it.

**My first real estate deal**

A real estate deal is any wholesale transaction where you receive the title, or a rehab where you sell the home to a buyer and get paid at closing. I would not consider being a bird dog and finding a property a deal. Some people might say that finding an address and giving it to an investor then making like $500 is a deal. I think that's just part of making a deal happen. A real deal is when you buy or sell a property and at the end, the title company hands you a check in your name. The proof is in the pudding is what people would say. You can say you've done all these deals and this and that but nothing matters until you show the proof of a check and the title documents. That proves that you did a real deal. It's a dog eat dog world so when you talk about doing something big, you better back it up. Because the people that want to see you fail, will bash on you and always want you to prove everything you're doing. I know some people won't care what other people think and I don't either. I really don't care about anybody's opinion or what they say about me. Because I will keep going no matter what they say or do to me. I would never give up or give in to their hate. But I love proving people wrong because I feel that's what everybody wants to do when everybody says they couldn't do something. You need those little accomplishments to prove those people wrong. I'm not saying to talk trash or say you're better than somebody. I'm saying to just show your accomplishments when they happen because there are so many people who want to see you fail but also so many people who want to see you win.

So, when you start doing more deals and getting that success, post on social media how you are doing and what's happening. Don't brag, just promote your accomplishments. Especially when you do it on social media where you know those haters are hiding and watching to see if you would succeed. Once you do this, almost 100% of the time those people will go away because you did it, you succeeded. And you'll get new amazing people in your life who support you and will continue to support your success. I always love seeing people around me succeed and achieve their dreams. I would rather see my friends and family do better than me. Because when I see everybody working hard and succeeding around me, it motivates me to work even harder. But not everybody can accomplish everything they say they will. It's a hard and lonely journey that you will most likely go on by yourself until you find other people on the same path. Even then, everybody's goals and destination will be different than yours. That's why you need to be ready to work by yourself, eat by yourself and just overall survive by yourself. Learn to only rely on yourself and nobody else.

To quit your job and start a business is mentally challenging. You're quitting guaranteed money to go out on a limb on something you think will work and from which you want to make a living. You're creating a business around something you love and praying you will be able to do your own deals that produce income. But hey, once the ball starts rolling keep feeding the business and it will blow up massively.

Of course, it all really starts with that first deal. That is what starts that fire inside you and gets you pushing hard. Doing deals keeps you motivated to do even more deals and make even more money. When you first launch your business, you will start with a whole lot of motivation. Everybody's hot off the line but it's how you stay motivated that counts. I was hot off the line when I first began too, then I started losing motivation. I will admit it was hard to keep going when I saw no change in income or lifestyle. When you live the same day over and over and you keep driving the same car, meeting the same people and having the same bank account, it can soon get discouraging. I was feeling down during some points but my friends and family kept me motivated.

I was consistently doing little things to reassure what I was doing was worth it and it kept me on track. I tried to watch some motivational videos every day and listen to real estate podcasts. I looked at people who were successful in real estate and all these homes I wanted to buy. I drove to dealerships and sat in the cars I dreamed about. I drove to neighborhoods of where I wanted to live. I just surrounded myself with the things I wanted to have and what I would get if I worked hard enough in real estate. Every time I did this, my motivation to work harder increased exponentially and I worked like I never had worked before. I think staying motivated is a huge part of achieving. If you're not motivated, then, why do it?

Once you figure out how to stay motivated, you will become an unstoppable train. Everybody has different ways to stay consistent. The ways I do it won't work for everybody because not everybody has the same idea of being successful and what they want to achieve. Right before I closed my first deal in real estate, while I was still in high school I was feeling super down. I was juggling all the responsibilities of graduating and completing all these things I needed to do to graduate. I had all these people cramming all this info of going to college and what I was doing with my life. I didn't announce what I was doing. Teachers and students kept asking me if I was going to college or not. I said I'm not going to college or a university and everybody just looked at me funny. I never said, "I'm not going to college because I'm a self-employed 18-year-old who is operating his own real estate business and I never want to go to college or be employed." Why? Because nobody would understand what I was doing and just keep asking questions. Almost every single day in my senior year I heard the word college and it made me sick. I hated hearing that word because I never understood getting a loan for $50k+, paying towards that for four years just to get into a job that pays you $12 an hour and you can't pay off the college debt until 20 years later. You're starting your life straight out of school and you want to go thousands of dollars into debt? I always thought I did good in math but I could never get those numbers work in my head. You just couldn't convince me that going to college would be more beneficial to me than becoming a self-employed entrepreneur. There are only a few professions I think you need to go to college to learn. These would include becoming a doctor, nurse or some sort of surgeon. There are only a few professions you need to go to college for, the rest you can go into the real world to learn how to do them or become that person. But I didn't want to become a doctor or a surgeon. Ever since I was young I knew I wanted to make an unlimited amount of money by myself. I knew I wanted to do whatever I wanted to make money and I didn't want to work for someone else. I hate seeing my family go away every day working a 9-5 then coming home just to eat and sleep. I wanted to live a life where I could see my friends and family whenever I wanted. I wanted to create a life where my kids will see me every single day and will always get to spend time with me. Spending time with my family is something I work hard for every day. This is a lot of people's motivation but this has always been my motivation since I was a little boy. I've been unemployed since I was 17 years old. Crazy, right? As I write this book now I'm 19 years old and feeling great. I was always doing a little business growing up from car detailing to reselling Craigslist and yard sales items. I was never fully committed though. I still worked a job because I wanted that guaranteed money every week to keep going. Honestly, I was scared to go full self-employed and work for myself. I was scared I would never make it and I wouldn't see any money. I felt like I would fail and go back to working my 9-5 which I never wanted to do.

The biggest mistake I made was waiting until I was ready and the moment was right to work for myself 100%. Since I wouldn't make the jump myself, God jumped in and did it for me. What I mean by that is when I left my job at 17 years old for a two-week vacation, I came back thinking I would find another job but I didn't. The Lord made it so nobody would hire me and I couldn't find a job. I was promised a job at a certain bank when I came back from my vacation but it was filled. They had lied to me. I applied everywhere for a few months and nobody called me back, gave me an interview or even showed interest in me. In the meantime, I was still going through school trying to get by with what money I had left and stretching it as far as I could. I felt down and out for the count.

Nobody would hire me or even give me a shot. That's when I knew I needed to make the jump and go for it. Make the jump to become self-employed and work for myself 100%. This was it, I'm not going back to any job and I will work for myself. I will admit that I was scared and didn't know what to do. Before I always had a plan on going to work every day and waiting for the right moment to become self-employed but now I felt hopeless and lost. I had no idea what to do or where to go. No guidance or support around me except from my friends and family who only wanted me to get a job. Nobody thought I could do it. My friends and family supported me but nobody really believes it until you show it. My family also knew I'd do something with money because I always loved selling things as a kid and making a dollar was exciting. So, after I couldn't find any job and no place would hire me, I just sat back and thought about what to do next. God was telling me to go for it. He was giving me the sign that I didn't needed to go to another 9-5 slave job. God told me that this is my time and I need to go self-employed and make my own money. No job deserved me and I was ready to move on to the bigger and better things in life. So, I looked around everywhere I could to see what career I wanted exactly and something I could do by myself. No boss. Just me working for myself and making my own dough. It had to involve some sort of buying and selling because that's what I loved doing and that was the most profitable.

At first I continued to do my car detailing business on a little bigger scale. I did some marketing online and did a few more details with customers that way. I posted all over Craigslist and told all of my friends/family. But I wasn't getting anywhere because I didn't make enough money to scale up my marketing and get all different kinds of marketing tools.

One day, I was looking online and found something about making a quick $10k by wholesaling houses. This instantly caught my attention and I spent all night researching and finding out precisely what wholesaling houses was and what exactly made it so easy. So, for the next couple of weeks I blocked everything out and just studied hard on this real estate career. Once I found out how quick and how much money you could make, I knew this was the answer. This was it. I found the thing I wanted to do and what I was going to achieve success and being my own boss. I continued to do my detailing while I studied every day and night on real estate. I studied during school which is part of the reason why I did so poorly my senior year. I was focused and I had tunnel vision. I had my eye on success and nothing else mattered. School and my part-time car washing gig were just small parts of my daily routine. Real estate was the thing om which I was really focusing all my energy. I had my blinders on and my focus was intense. I wanted my first deal so badly to prove all these haters wrong and prove myself right. I knew I could make this work and nothing else mattered. I worked on this every single day studying the different ways to find and conduct my first deal.

    Of course, really the first thing I found was to post Craigslist ads and drive for dollars. These are some of the most basic and free ways to find real estate deals. So, I posted Craigslist ads about buying houses. I had no team and had no idea what to do when I got a real person to call me. But every day I still posted all these Craigslist ads on as many accounts as I could because I knew I could make a deal happen from using Craigslist if I posted so many ads. Eventually somebody would respond and I would achieve it. But I was still scared and nervous when somebody would call me. But somebody sent me an email one day asking me what deals I had and what I was doing. His name was Andrew Lebaron and he asked to meet up with me to find out if I could help him and he could help me. I said okay and had no idea what to expect because this was my first real estate related meeting.

    A few days later we met at a Chipotle and he bought me lunch which I'll never forget because he was the nicest person I'd met in real estate and continues to be one of the nicest and greatest persons I've ever met in my life so far. I'd met some great people before but he had a genuinely good soul and cared about helping other people besides himself. We had a terrific meeting and we have been great friends ever since that day. After he brought me under his wing with his company True Freedom Achievers, I worked underneath and watching everything he did and how he did it. He gave me the courage to wake up and work hard every single day because he believed that I would be successful and do some deals. This guy who barely knew me, said he believed in me because he saw something inside me. He saw the fire inside me burning to be successful. He saw it and he was the exact person I needed in my life at that time.

By the time I realized it, he was my mentor. I had my own mentor and it felt amazing to have somebody to watch over and help me do better. Every day Andrew taught me something new. I went on appointments with him, drove him and learned the basics and how this business actually worked. I got a few deals through Craigslist and Driving for Dollars but they kept falling through when it got time to close. There would be liens on the property or they would foreclose faster than I could close, sellers being dishonest and just all this stuff happening where I couldn't make a deal happen or make a deal work. It was very frustrating. I couldn't make a deal happen and I had every doubt in the world on why this wouldn't work and I let some negative thoughts into my mind. That's something you should never do and I started doing that because I couldn't close these deals. But I listened to some podcasts and some of those amazing motivational videos on YouTube and got back in it. I was back in the game once I found some motivation and hit it hard again. I started to look back at all the things I was doing to make those deals come to the table but just couldn't close. I applied all those skills and things that were working to my next big come up. Then something came to me one day.

Our company was doing anywhere around 20-40 properties per month by wholesaling.

And I noticed some of them just sit there and don't move for a while. They have a really big buyer's list of people looking to purchase rehabs. Probably one of the biggest lists in Arizona, I think judging by the number of people who are signed up and how fast the deals get sold. But as I saw some of the properties not move, I asked and they would say they it's a hard deal or it's for a specific type of buyer. Sometimes it was a high priced property or a unique property in which they needed to add square feet. in order to make it a deal. So, I started posting the properties all over Craigslist that just sat on the website. I marked each one of the properties up just a little bit. Just a couple thousand. Nothing too crazy because otherwise it would make the deal not make sense and look overpriced. By then I was already posting ads saying I buy houses and all this so I was building a buyer's list because a lot of buyers would call me looking for deals. I had a list of buyers I would send these deals to every day and nobody would respond. They would always ignore the email and never call me back. When I would call them, they would always blow me off and give me some lame excuses. I got tired of them saying all this garbage to me every day. Every day getting rejected and laughed at saying I didn't know what I was doing and I didn't know how to do this and that. But no matter what was said to me or how many times I got rejected, I continued to post these properties on Craigslist because I knew eventually one day somebody would bite. Then it happened. I remember the day so clearly. I was just walking out of the gym, maybe $50 in my bank account, and I received a phone call.

This person was calling about one of my properties I had on Craigslist and asked me some more questions. So, I pulled up the house on my phone as soon as I could to give him accurate information. He said he was very interested in it and asked me a few more questions on it, which I answered because I had my phone out. He said that he wanted to offer me full price and wanted to know how much earnest was. My heart was racing! He verbally agreed to buy the property so I told him it was a $3k deposit and he said that was fine. I arranged a meeting the next day in Tempe. I called my buddy Andrew and asked him to send me the contract. The next day he sent it to me and I met the buyers at a local Starbucks in Tempe (you will do a lot of deals and meeting at Starbucks! I can promise that because it's a great place to meet people). Once I met the buyers we spoke for a little bit about how this is their first deal and all their background from going to working a 9-5 job to being self-employed flipping homes. It was a cool story and they showed me the earnest money. I just took a picture of it because they were willing to drop it off at the title agency on their way back home. They lived in Phoenix and it was on the way. As soon as they signed the contract I shook their hand and proceeded to go back home. My heart was racing and I felt amazing. It sounds funny but this was my first deal and it was signed. All they had to was sign and I got paid. I went home and told my family. Two weeks later we closed and I drove to the title office myself and picked up the check with my best friend Donovan.

It was amazing and the first person I told was the most important person in my life, my mom. I couldn't believe I finally did it and it felt amazing holding that $3k check in my hands (this was my mark up for the property). It wasn't huge but it was good enough to get me started and keep me going for my marketing! I used the money the best way I could. I spaced it out and spent it wisely so I could use it as fuel to keep moving forward at a progressive rate. I didn't waste it on watches, clothes or anything that wasn't for my business. After I cashed the check and it became 100% real after holding the money in my hands, I spent that day just thinking back on all the hard work, all the struggles I went through to get to this point. All the ups and downs I experienced along the way. Then I realized that this business was going to change my life. I've never grown so much in such a short period of time in anything else I've ever done in life. This was my first deal in the big boy business and I felt great. I knew it wouldn't be my last. But I promise your first deal in any business will be the hardest deal, but you will grow the most from that deal and the rest after that will come a lot easier if you just stay dedicated and work hard every day.

Doing that deal was hard. It takes dedication to wake up every day, be willing to not make money every day until you got that deal and made the checks. You have to wake up and just be about it every single day. Whether you feel good or not. Do something that puts you ahead at least 1% every day. But no matter if your first deal comes easy or hard, you have to keep the train chugging along. It's easy to get distracted from the small successes but you must keep your eye on the big goals. Keep focused on the bigger things you're working for. Work hard and celebrate the small victories but don't forget why you started and why you're doing this. Stay consistent and the deals will happen. It's easy to get unfocused and unmotivated but I promise whoever is reading this right now, it will get better and you will make it. Everything will be okay. Be willing to give something if you want a return. Stay consistent on that action every day and everything will be okay. I can promise you from my past experiences.

**Chapter Five**

**Hater Goggles**

**"Don't let haters get in the way of your dream."-Caleb Maddix**

This chapter is all about haters/ the people who don't support you, throw you down and just hate you and everything you are doing. I'll talk about how to block these people out and how to keep moving forward even when you feel like the world is against you and everything you're doing. You'll have to put on your "hater goggles" and keep pushing forward. Standing out is very hard for most when we were taught to fit in with other people. Our generation always taught us how to blend in but never how to stand out. I think it's a shame for all the people who have such beautiful gifts but get hated for being different. The people who are different and ambitious, are usually the ones who change the world. The people who show any sort of individuality in school or in a social group, are bashed because they aren't the same. In school, it's the hardest. Middle school and high school are usually the toughest to fit in and be popular. All the kids who wear different clothes, listen to different music, too skinny, too fat, a different race, don't speak English well, don't socialize well get bashed the most. It's because they don't fit in in, they aren't wearing the newest clothes or speaking the same way as everyone else. Other kids are mean. They will bully, spit on you or just plain ignore you.

I think this one of the hardest things you can put a young teen/adult through. In middle school, they are expecting to make all these friends but end up with nobody talking to them and just getting treated like trash. Then their parents expect them to go to every class and pass with As.

These parents set such a high standard without realizing what is going on emotionally with their children. If you don't know why your kid is failing but they are coming home depressed and upset every day, go back and figure out what's going on. Know your children and figure out what's going on. All these parents expect their children to do the best in school and get straight A's but they never really understand their kid's feelings and how they live day to day. You will never really know what your kids or family members are going though. Reach down to an emotional level and you will then realize what's going on. Get in their shoes for a day because you can't expect all those good grades, trophies and awards when you don't understand what these people are going through every day. It's very hard to focus on school and doing well when you face a deluge of negative comments every day and so much negative energy in your life. It's honestly one the hardest things to do in life to keep moving forward when nobody is there supporting you and bringing that positive energy in your life and when all you face is the negative energy.

    I experienced this firsthand. I was hated for being chunkier in middle school and not being athletic in sports or PE. I didn't run the fastest mile and I couldn't lift the heaviest weights. When we had assemblies awarding students for being excellent, I never got any. I was never awarded for being the best student in class, attendance or having the best grades. I had amazing friends but we weren't a part of the popular club. I didn't date any popular or beautiful girls, so people always judged me for who I spent my time with and dated. People always questioned me and what I was doing all the time. They would judge me for not going to the school dances because I didn't feel comfortable going, they judged me for not being able to afford the fancy lunch but they didn't care about the struggles at home. They judged me for not having a brand-new phone or a new gaming system. All these kids judging me every single day and going through all this negative energy every day at school.

    Most days I didn't want to go to school at all just because I knew all the things I was going to experience. That's why many teens dread going to class, especially the ones who are different. Why be forced to go to a setting where all they do is hate you and you feel like garbage every time you're there? Why would any logical person do that? As adults, if we know somewhere is a bad environment we choose not to go to that place but as young teens in middle school and high school, we are forced into these environments. If you look back and visualize your experience in school, would you go if you had the choice? Or would you change schools and go somewhere you fit in and are accepted as you are. Many people would go back and change everything they did and all the things they involved themselves in.

But what you must realize is that because of the actions you took, it made you who you are today. If you could go back and make all the right decisions, we would never fail and never learn. People who fail never learn. If all you did was succeed, you would never learn what not to do from the failures and you wouldn't be a structured/experienced person. Every time you fail, you learn a new way not to do something. You learn from the mistakes then rebuild and try again. If you fail again, you will continually learn and this will start to build you into an amazing person. Nobody who is successful succeeded on their first attempt and became a millionaire. No, they continually failed and failed until they found the correct path to be on to become that millionaire. Once they found the path, they followed it until they got bigger and better. They failed along the way and learned from those mistakes every single time. That's why you are meant to be on a certain path and you can't fight with it. The sooner you accept that the path you're on is meant for you, the sooner you will go with the flow and get to the top. Realizing and accepting it is the final step before becoming successful. Accept the failures and go with the flow because everything happens for a reason and everything will happen to put you in the perfect spot at the perfect time so you can accomplish everything you want at that moment. God is putting you on a specific path for a reason.

Everything in your life happens for some reason no matter if it's bad or good. These problems get placed in your life for some reason either to motivate you to push harder or maybe to give you a reality. Oftentimes you think you are invincible so life hands you a hard challenge to see what you can do and keep you on your toes. I love when I get problems or things don't go as planned because I use that to fuel me to go even harder. It also makes me realize what I've got and how fast I could lose it.

There needs to be that perfect balance of appreciating everything around you and how perfect your life is going and a little bit of fear/insecurity of what could happen if you mess around. Stay consistent and on your path. But just be aware of the bumps that come along with the road. No road was created perfect and that's what you should expect along your journey of success. The road will have some very high ups where you feel on top of the world, everybody will cherish you and the ground you walk on. You feel like nothing will hurt you or bring you down. But the road will also bring some of the lowest of the lows where you feel unmotivated, defeated, destroyed and no chance of succeeding. But I can honestly promise you, once you get through these low lows, you will see some of the highest highs and the biggest accomplishments you've ever had in your entire life. Just keep going through these hard times and you will enjoy the good times for a long while if you stay on the path and stay working smart. Don't slack and stay on that path! The harder and smarter you work, the longer you will get to enjoy these amazing highs.

People won't support what you're doing. By people, I mean those closest around you including friends and family. People closest to you are the hardest ones to convince of your choices. They support you up until they change their mind. They will support you verbally, thinking you will never do it and when you get ready to accomplish it, they start hating and saying you shouldn't do it. Why is that? These people will always support you up until you act and do the things you said you were going to do. It's like when you ask your friend if you should lose weight and of course they say yes because you're a little fat/ little overweight. They say yeah you should work out and they give you some suggestions on what to do. Then you start working out and getting a little more in shape. Maybe you start exceeding the physical condition of your friend. Your friend will start asking questions on how you're doing it and what's the trick. Then your friend will start talking shit once you surpass them and get in even better shape than them. People will always motivate and support you until you pass or do better than them. It's the same with anything whether it be business, working out, reading, driving, anything. No matter what you do, you will always have people supporting you all the way and people who will hate you no matter how successful or how well you do. There are so few people telling you to do it but there is also a bunch of people telling you to not do it or save your money and not invest it. You're ready to accelerate then there's those people in the background putting mental pressure on the brakes trying to slow you down and stop you altogether. These people that are "haters" can come in all shapes, forms and different times in your life. The people can come in when you are doing well or they can come at you when you're doing bad to try and push you down even harder. You see, when people hate, it's because you're living one of their dreams or doing something they didn't have the balls to do. You're doing something these people thought about and dreamt of doing. That's all haters are. People living in the past not taking action to do the things you're doing. Deep down they are hating because they hate the fact that you did something they couldn't or didn't even attempt. For example, your friend and you work together at some crappy 9-5 job. After a while, a business opportunity comes around where you can invest your money and start a business or own a part of one. This business opportunity is for anybody who has enough money. And to have enough money, it takes more than what you have saved but your friend has more than enough saved up. Only your friend has enough money to invest but you're still shorthanded. Your friend talks about it every day at work and raves about all the good things that could come of it and how much money you guys could make. He gushes about the house he would buy, the car he would buy and the women that would come around once he was rich. But he's scared. He's too afraid to leave his safe 9-5 job and go for it. He's afraid to jump and make his dreams come true and all the things he takes apart, are just words. He isn't taking action, but he talks about it every day.

On the other hand, you suggest that perhaps you will get another job and come up with the money to invest. Of course, being your friend, he says yes you should and motivates you to put all your money into the business idea. Now in the back of your friend's head, he's thinking that you won't get another job because you don't have the time and you don't have the dedication to save up your money. Then while your friend is out partying every weekend on his free time and wasting his saved money, you go out and get a job on the weekends but you didn't tell him. You keep it a secret so you can surprise him when you get enough money to jump into the business venture together. A month or two goes by and you finally have enough money saved, so you go to your friend and show him the cash and explain the second job you picked up. Your friend acts surprised and stands amazed about what you did. He now realizes you are serious and changes his attitude a little bit to show that. You suggest that the two of you put your money together and go for the business venture that closes soon. He makes up 100 million excuses about why he can't and what if doesn't work. Blah blah blah blah. Basically, he's scared to do what needs to be done when he's faced with the decision to actually make all his dreams come true. So, you say you'll do it anyway to see if it's real and to try and convince your friend to join in.

 A couple weeks go by and your friend still hasn't joined and the window for joining is about to close. You show some success already and start making an incredible return. So, you still try to convince your friend to join and he still says he's scared. You're doing so well that you quit the job that you and your friend work at together. A few more weeks go by and your friend sees all the success on your Facebook, the new car you bought and just all the new opportunities presenting themselves because of the jump you took. Immediately your friend calls you and tries to join but it's too late. You try explaining but he just gets upset and mad at you. You're confused because this is one of your closest friends but he's yelling at you and he's genuinely angry. He hangs up and you don't talk for months.

You're successful now with a good amount of money, amazing house and a beautiful wife. You're out shopping and there you see your friend, working at the same job half a year ago, and he just stares at you with regret and anger. You walk with your beautiful wife out to your new car and he just stares at you. Then a few days later you see him talking trash about you saying how you cheated or you got lucky, some BS like that. He is now officially a hater. Somebody who was once a really good friend of yours, maybe even a best friend is now a hater. Now this isn't everybody. Not everybody near you will turn into a hater but most them will. If they don't turn and they stay supporting you and love seeing you win, you hold tight onto those friends. They will stick by your side for a long time. The best thing you can do is to keep on doing you. Keep doing what you're doing because when a lot of people are hating you, that means you're doing something right. When you blend in and act like everybody else, everybody will like you and show affection towards you. These people may not really like you, but they like you now because you are just like them. When you go through your success journey, you will filter out all the fake people and you'll reveal the real people that really support you.

During my senior year in high school I started going through this phase of filtering everybody out. Once I started standing out by getting into real estate and having a little money, people around me began acting differently and treated me differently too. All these kids I grew up with and knew personally, stopped talking to me or ignored me entirely. This is when I knew I was doing something right. It dawned on me who my real friends were and who stayed by my side when I became more successful towards graduation. I filtered out anybody who didn't support me or hated on me in any way. I didn't want those types of people in my life and neither do you. Filter all those people out who don't support you or understand why you're doing what you're doing. Don't be afraid to do it no matter who that person is to you. Because this is the new you and if they can't accept it, see ya later, hater. Your business and future self will thank you.

How do you block these people out and ignore the major haters in your life? How do you use these people to your advantage to blow up in your business and succeed even more while they continue to hate you?

Believe it or not, haters can benefit you. They can help you grow your business and even make more money. We already went over the fact that no matter what you do in life or in business, you will have haters. Whatever you do you will have some people hating you. You will most likely have more haters than supporters. Which is okay. Trust me it is. Because you can use these people to your advantage without them even knowing it. As an entrepreneur, you will need to look at every problem and see how you can create a solution.

That's how self-employed people make money. We see a problem, find a solution and make a living. That's how anybody can make a living doing what they love. Just find a problem people face day to day and figure out how to solve it/get it done faster. So, what do you do when you see all these haters around you giving you all this attention? How can you use all this attention to your advantage? You see, when people hate you, your name is in their mouths all the time or posted all over social media. Whatever way they talk crap, they are using your name and blasting it out everywhere. What you need to learn to do is get MORE haters. Because the more haters you have, the more people are talking about you. These haters will tell their friends or family about you then look you up online to find facts about the crap they are talking. Most of the time these haters will convince their friends and family to hate you as well, but when their friends tell their friends and tell their friends, somebody is bound to like you and turn into a supporter. Which In turn, these people that turn into supporters will end up buying your programs, books, etc., just about anything you have for sale about your success. Because no matter what, not everybody will hate you. Some of those people will be interested in you and how you got so successful. Which turns into profits because they are buying what your business is selling. Maybe they will even invest some money with you or tell some other great people about you and they will reach out to you. Some people will even offer services to you at a severe discount just so you do business with them. People will bring multiple opportunities to make even more money. Your life could even change just by having all those haters speak about you and say your name all over social media. Remember, just because it's negative attention, doesn't mean it's necessarily bad. Your income could skyrocket just by getting more opportunities through your haters' friends. All of this could happen just by people speaking about you. And guess what? This was all free. You didn't have to pay for these haters to talk about you and blast you all over social media. There are so many social media agencies that pay hundreds of thousands if not millions of dollars every month to try and get noticed. These businesses pay so much money every week praying their business name or idea will get saturate social media. While you just upset people, and make them uncomfortable enough to where they are posting all over social media about you.

Of course, while everybody is posting these different opinions about you, you will need to have tough skin to stick through it and not pay any attention to these people. Just let them keep talking while you sit back and count the cash. Sit back and watch your business explode all over the Internet and everybody knows who you are. Do things differently and stand out. In our recent election, Trump vs. Hillary, I'm not going to talk political but I'm just going to lay down some facts. Before this election even took place, I would say many people knew who Trump was. Everybody in business knew who he was. He came into the election weak. He came in with nobody voting for him or believing in him because he was so different and had all these goofy ideas. He didn't put any money into his marketing but instead raised most of the money through the people's support. Through everything I read, watched and viewed about Mr. Trump he was a great guy. Not very loud, just a great guy who loved business. I once read a story about him paying off a family's mortgage just because a man stopped to help Mr. Trump change a tire on his limo. All the actions he took like talking crazy and being brutally honest on camera put him back in the race. Talking about things people didn't want to talk about is what put Donald Trump in the race and put him ahead. Everybody loved how he was talking and how honest he was being. He was so different from all the other candidates in the way he spoke and just the way he did things. He was the richest but spent no money on his campaign. While Hillary spent over $200 million, mostly her own money. I honestly believe that he recognized the potential of the haters and used it to his advantage. He knew that the more outrageous he became and the more honest he was, more people would notice him and the social media would revolve around him. And it worked. During the election, you couldn't get away from seeing a Trump video or a Trump tweet. He was honestly everywhere. And at the same time, he wasn't paying for any of that marketing. It was all just word of mouth from people posting about him and talking about him. While all this was happening, the other candidates couldn't dump money into their marketing fast enough to even compete with Donald. They couldn't stand out like he did and just kind of faded away because no attention was going to them. Look who up ended up winning. Trump. It's because people had so much emotion involved with him because he was everywhere. Some people learn how to use everything that comes into their life to their advantage. These people are some of the most successful people you will meet. Like Tai Lopez said, catch the trends before they happen. As an entrepreneur, you will be solving problems all the time but if you want to be super successful, learn how to catch trends before they happen. Tai preaches this because it's so true. If you can predict something before it happens, you can make so much/become so successful. Why? Because it's basically predicting the future. Take for example the crash of 2006. Terrible time for a lot of people. Why? Because nobody was prepared or ready for it. Most people thought they would live their happy life forever and nothing bad would ever happen. But about 1% of the people weren't even affected. Heck, they were happy. Because the 1% of people who were successful, were ready and predicted the crash that was going to happen. They knew when it was and they all prepared. Not being prepared is the worst thing that can happen to you. All the wise people who saw the future and predicted the crash, became even richer by buying businesses, houses, land, etc. They moved their equity around and bought things when they were very cheap. Pennies on the dollar basically. When they bought all those properties they either remodeled them and sold them, or are holding onto them as rentals. Or even now they could still be holding onto them because they know what they are worth and waiting till we get to the top of the market again then sell them before the next crash.

    This won't all come at once being an entrepreneur. This is something you must train your mind to do. Study the market and predict what's happening next. Hold onto everything until you're ready to make a huge move and put everything in. Make little moves until you can make the big one. I remember Gary V talking about how he saved for 10-15 years until he saw an opportunity to invest all the money he had earned. Most people fail by investing everything they have at the first shiny object they see. Don't be afraid to sit back and be patient. Your time will come and when it does, jump on it and give it everything you've got. But don't be afraid. Don't get to your time to shine and not go for it. Once you recognize your true potential, go for it. Don't let anybody or anything hold you back. Continue to press forward through all the hateful/mean people in your journey. Keep going no matter what anybody says or what happens in your success journey. Keep grinding while everybody is partying. Stay on the path you feel is right and It will always pay off. Be patient and the wait will be worth it. That's what makes us entrepreneurs and regular people stand out. Entrepreneurs are a different type of person and I guarantee it. We think, act and do different than regular people. Don't be afraid of the change that will come, accept it and you will grow into this new amazing person. Once you become an official entrepreneur, you will do everything differently and the things that didn't make sense before now will. You will think of everything as a business and you will be thinking about how to help people and change lives. It's a completely different way of living. I can't wait till all of you get out of the 9-5 mindset and jump into the entrepreneur mindset. You won't regret it and I promise you'll never go back. This was one of the chapters you can apply to your life right away and use to your advantage. Anybody can do it but so few people actually do. If you apply everything I just said in this one chapter, I can almost guarantee your life will start to change and everything in it. Pay attention and watch everything take shape. I wish you guys nothing but the best of luck.

# Chapter Six

## The Infamous Phone Call

*"There will be a day soon when you have to make your big move. When that day comes, be bold."* Tai Lopez

Now I will finally talk about my infamous phone call that led me to making the $8,000, and everything it took to make that deal possible and how I'm using the money to make more money/opportunities. And how you can use your big deals' money to create much more wealth and open doors you never had been able to open before. You can use $8,000 to make a whole lot more money than that. Once you go through a struggle of using zero money to close deals, then you go to making big money, deals will start coming in a little easier and quite a bit faster. The money helps grease the track for the deal train. It helps move everything a lot faster. Money always helps when you know how to use it correctly. Try not to be foolish with it and put yourself on a strict budget of what to spend for extra personal things and what to save for your business. Getting a bigger amount of money than you're used to can make your head spin. You'll want to buy unnecessary things that don't help you. Watches, shoes, clothes, etc. When you make this money, be prepared to spend some on your business and to save the rest until you need it. Don't think just because you have all this money that you can spend it however you choose. You will need to make wise financial decisions because the choices you make will determine the fate of your business.

The call I made to make the deal possible. What exactly is the $8,000 phone call? I've had a lot of people ask me why I titled this book as I did. Many think it was because I made a lot of money on one deal and now I know everything. Most think that just because I did a few deals that I want to be a mentor and that I'm an expert in real estate.

This is not the case at all. By no means am I pro. I don't think anybody is a pro, and if you think you are, you are foolish. You should always be learning and growing. I don't think I will ever be the best in real estate because I will always be learning more and growing more as a business. I believe I will do well in real estate but never master it. This book was not created to boast or to brag about my accomplishments. It was created to inspire the youth and motivate those around me to do whatever they want. Nothing is stopping anybody from doing what they love. I want this book to inspire you to get up and start your very own business. Quit whatever is stopping you from achieving your goal. Get up and just go do it! Quit making all the excuses and just do it. Get off the couch or put down the video games and do it. It took a lot of hard work and dedication to make this deal happen. It took a lot of heart, hard work and sweat equity. It didn't just happen on a phone call. Everything leading up to this very moment took almost a year. It was a real struggle. This wasn't my first deal and it certainly won't be my last. I've had so many people assume this is my first deal and that's why I'm writing this book. It's not my first deal and that's not why I wrote the book.

I did close a wholesale deal for $8,200 and everything that happened during that time inspired me to write a book. It took many hours of hustling, long nights and lots of failure. I failed so many times to close a deal it's crazy. So many contracts ignored, so many doors slammed in my face, phone calls hung up on, just so much rejection it's insane. But each time I heard a no brought me closer to another deal and I grew each and every time. I would always learn how to do something or how not to. I learned what people liked hearing and what they did not want to hear. I've made so many mistakes that when I look back now I can clearly see all the deals I passed on or that were rejected, and I realize that I could have possibly made a deal if I had done things differently. But you can't look back, only forward! If you look back and think back, you'll start going backwards. Don't ever do that. Only go forward and grow every day. If you grow just 1% every day, at the end of the year you'll have grown by 365%. What kind of person do you think you'll by the time you reach 100% let alone 365%? You will think differently, act differently and learn differently. Each and every "no" I heard helped me to grow a little bit. Don't take it personally every time every time you get rejected or hear the word no. Learn from what you might have done wrong and keep moving forward. It hurt me a lot when I first started in business and heard the word no more times than yes. I learned to take the word no and keep going. Once I learned that every no I heard was one step closer to yes, I got used to hearing the word no. I grew each and every time until I finally started hearing yes. I learned so much leading up to this point and such a parade of ideas marched through my head that I just felt I had to share them.

    I had done deals prior to this one, but this deal was special. I did a lot of learning up until this point and I felt different after the deal was done. I knew I had grown a lot in my business and just to look back and see all that was accomplished was crazy. I used different resources and different means to make this deal happen. New marketing techniques that I was experimenting with paid off. Trying something new and having it work is the greatest feeling I think.

    During this time, I met new people, made my name heard and gained more respect. People started knowing who I was and what I was doing. I began to get people to message me with deals and wanting to work with me. I had a lot of people message me for tips and tricks. I never thought people would be asking me for help when I was just a small fry not too long ago. Now folks look up to me and come to me for help. I realized that you can't do this by yourself. You can go only go so far by yourself, you can go much farther if you have a solid team all pitching in and making it work. The more people I added to my team and the more people who assisted me in finding deals, the easier it become. Once I figured this out, I made concerted efforts to talk to as many people as possible trying to add value to everyone so we could all work together and become successful.

All business and real estate people have the same goal, to be successful. If you're not willing to meet new people and grow your team, you shouldn't be in business. I don't know one successful person who did it all on their own. Everybody has had help and a team behind them to get so far ahead. Don't be self-made, be team made! That's when everybody becomes successful together and we are all happy. Trust me, the sooner you realize that you can get to your goal so much faster with the help of other people, you'll try to get as many as possible on your team. You need to pick the best candidates who can help speed up the progress in each area of your business. Somebody who specializes in sales, another in calls, another in meetings, etc. Since everybody is on the same mission, you can all help each other out and grow together. If someone is going through a hard time, you can help them get through it. You can all succeed together. For me, seeing everybody on my team win is the best feeling you can have. It shows how far you guys have come and how much farther your team can go when everybody helps each other. Plus, when everybody is working together, you start building a loyal team that will do anything for you. You can have as many friends and teammates as you want but only the loyal people matter. You don't want your team leaving you and going with a competitor. Just keep a good relationship with them, check up with them and see how they are performing and see if they need anything. If something is holding them back from succeeding, talk with them and help them get past it, because when they succeed, you succeed. Treat them the same as if it's your success on the line.

    I try to help as many people as possible. But many of these people come to me asking for the secret or magic way of doing deals. The only secret is hard work! That's it, just work hard towards a goal and take massive action. Only then will you achieve what you want. I could give you all the tips in the world needed to do your first deal but it won't matter unless you get off your butt and do something about it! I learned a lot taking that advice. They always say once you learn, teach. That's exactly why I wrote this book, to teach and inspire everybody. I always saw everybody I learned from teach once they got a little better just so all the people around them started winning. My goal with this book was just to hopefully inspire the people who feel down or those who are close to starting. I want everybody who reads this book to get up and take some sort of action that will change how you think or live. Whether it be reading a book/more books, quitting your job, asking for a promotion or meeting the love of your life. It all begins with you acting and being proactive. If you want reaction, you must first take action. Everything you do has some sort of effect on your life. Your life won't change if you're not doing different things and trying to consistently change.

What led me to that phone call? I closed deals prior to this deal for $8,200. They were smaller deals that didn't profit me nearly as much as this one; also, none of them were this easy. It's crazy. You work so hard then suddenly it comes easily. You could work 100 hours and the joy doesn't come until 101 hours. You could work so hard and grind every single day then one day it will all just fall into place and all your hard work will pay off. That will be the best day of your life. You'll feel better than ever and you'll finally know all those hours paid off. But I was busting my butt trying to get one of the more profitable deals. Anything over $5k-$6k through a wholesale deal was big for me (at the time, of course). I've now got my eyes set on much bigger wholesale deal profits. A big deal for me now would be $15k+. I was making cold calls every day praying somebody would sell me their house at a good enough discount to where my whole team made a nice profit and I cleared over $6k. I was out "driving for dollars", writing down addresses and leaving notes at every house I saw with potential. I probably skip traced 60+ addresses per week and called all of them. I knocked on every door, every day that looked good or promising to rehab. I put out so many bandit signs every weekend t only to have the city tear them down. I was spending most of the money I had on my real estate business. Fliers, business cards, gas to drive around looking at properties, vehicle repairs, etc. I would spend a few thousand then close a deal for a few thousand. I was just breaking even all the time money wise. I was mainly just learning and gaining experience from every deal. Which wasn't bad but I would have liked to make more money to spend a little on myself and then the rest on the business. Who wouldn't? So, after hustling every day I would call all those skip-traced properties and post a few more ads on Craigslist. Doing stuff consistently that would better my chances of getting a big deal. I was always taught to not worry about the money, just worry about solving the problem and the money will come. I am a true and firm believer in investing in things that solve problems or make people's lives easier. I know that if you invent something that makes people's lives way easier, gets stuff done faster or solves a common problem, the money will always come and you will be rich. No matter what it is, if it follows one of those things, you will have more than enough money and become successful. My mentor Andrew always told me to invest my time in myself and on other people who could help me get to where I want to be. He told me always to be networking and finding new people to talk to every day. So, that's exactly what I did. Even though I didn't feel comfortable just networking and talking because I didn't feel I was going to make money but I still did it. I started adding all kinds of real estate pros to my Facebook and essentially all my social media platforms. I figured once I had real estate and success all around me it would eventually rub off. I began talking to these people by message or even calling them directly to see how I could help them and how we could benefit each other. I was constantly trying to add value to every single person I met because why would these people teach me or help me for free unless I could add value to them? You wouldn't just give knowledge away for free when you worked so hard to learn that knowledge . So, if you could figure a way to scratch their back in exchange for the knowledge like bringing deals to them directly or maybe helping them some other way, it's a win win for both of you. If you can't think of a way to help them, just ask. Never be afraid to ask for something you really want. The sooner you learn this, the sooner you will become successful. By being truthful, people will almost always give you some sort of help. Just don't sound desperate. I've acquired a lot of knowledge simply by asking the questions when nobody else would and also by doing the hard work. That's the secret really, just do the things other people aren't willing to do so you can have the things the other people don't.

    Once I started to experience this firsthand and doing all these things that I didn't feel comfortable doing, my life began changing. I started to see growth day by day, and saw new people enter my life who assisted me in the process of closing deals. My team was growing and so was I. I felt as if I was growing into an entirely different person. My thinking started changing because I was hanging around and meeting people who thought entirely different than me. If you want to be a millionaire, you must think like one. You can't be rich and still thinking poor. Don't think about how you can pinch pennies -- be a boss and learn how to spend wisely. I also started using my team fully by using all available resources to create the most income. Our team had a huge buyers' list set up but it wasn't us personally emailing these people every time a property came out. We didn't follow up with them. We just waited for a call that would give us success. I felt it should've been more personal and more one on one with every single buyer. So, I began building my separate list of buyers that I was in touch with daily trying to find properties that met their needs. When I found a property, I knew exactly who to call. I had a personal connection with almost all these people. I searched for people who needed rehab/rental properties and I reached out to every single one of them. I grabbed their email and phone number from them, and then I would call each one of them to find out exactly what they wanted. When one of my team members got something under contract, I would send it to my buyers and then call them right afterwards explaining the deal. I would mark it up enough for myself to make a decent amount plus what my team made. Everybody was winning, and my buyers were happy that I was delivering properties.

Every night after a day of hustling I would send these buyers an email of all the properties my team had under contract, then follow up with them the next day. It was a great system and the people loved being so close and connected with me. They felt each deal was personal. These were people who weren't on our original email blast list so they couldn't see the original price and deal. I marked every deal up according to what made sense with margins. Typically, $3k-$4k per deal. I was feeling really good because this was just another way to position myself to make a deal happen and increase my income. If I couldn't land it big by buying the deal, I could make some good money on the back end by selling the deal to a buyer for a marked-up price. I was making these buyers feel important. I was always searching for buyers on every social media platform. Then I came across this huge buyer who rehabs and add values to each property by either adding square footage, bedrooms, amenities or something to make each property special. His name was Alex and I met him on Instagram. I already knew him from some other deals we ran into together but I finally reached out to him and followed him on Instagram asking him if there was any way I could help him so we could make deals happen together. He told me his criteria for properties and I searched my team's properties and I had one that was perfect for him. It was a higher priced property in a great part of Phoenix known as Arcadia. The property was hard to sell because it was priced at $350k cash. Many rehabbers can't come up with this much cash. But the ARV (after repair value) was over $600k with added square feet. I knew it was a killer deal with a huge return. So, I marked it up $8,500 and I was a little bit nervous because I felt it was kind of high. But with the amount of money he will make off this deal, I felt it was a good price. Before I sent it, I called him and told him about the property. He was very interested, so as soon as I got off the phone, I sent the deal to him. He immediately ran some numbers and was super interested. He asked me if I could meet him ay the house the next day and do a walk through. He was in California so I met with his partner the very next day and did a walk through with the homeowners still in the house. Setting this up is not very hard but it can be if you are dealing with homeowners who are not very fair and get upset easily.

    They were nice enough to let us in on such short notice. Always try to establish a great relationship with the homeowner because it make the deal work so much smoother. So, we got into the property and he did a complete walk through with his contractor looking where they could add square feet and tremendous amounts of value. I could tell by his expressions and the way he looked at the house that he saw dollar signs everywhere and wanted the property. He kept his cool then said his partner would be in touch with me.

I went on with my day and waited for him to call me. I didn't want to seem desperate so I just played the waiting game. It killed me because I knew he wanted the deal but now I was just waiting for his call. If he accepted the offer at that price I would make $8,500 with just a single phone call and an appointment at the house. He eventually called me towards the end of the day offering $3k less. I was kind of bummed because that meant I would only make $5k but I would still make out very well. I held my ground, though, because I knew what the deal was worth. I didn't lower my standards and I wasn't desperate to make the money. I told myself to hold out and not accept the offer. I knew it was worth more than what he offered. That's a very important lesson I've learned on my journey as well. Don't ever lower your standards to meet your reality. Work hard and keep your standards up and one day it will pay off. No matter what it is, never lower yourself to make your dreams work. Trust me, keep your head high and your standards the same. Anyway, I countered at $500 less than my original asking price and I offered to buy him lunch. He accepted within thirty minutes, then I sent him the contract for him to sign. My heart was racing and I was super excited. He signed the contract and sent it to me right away. Right after that I told him where and how much money to send me as the non-refundable earnest money deposit. For those of you who don't know what that is, it's just a deposit for the house to show he's serious about buying it. After he sends that, he has only a certain amount of time to pay for the property and close the deal. This deal was two weeks including weekends but he closed in about five days' total. The deposit protects our time being dedicated because we could've sold it in the meantime. So, if he didn't close on the said date we agreed on, he would lose the money he put down and it would go into our pockets and then we would look for another buyer. He sent the earnest money deposit within an hour to the title company. We closed on the deal that next Friday and I was going crazy every day because I'd done deals before that got to the title company and then the deal fell through. All I knew was that if I closed the deal, this would be my biggest to date.

 I continued to hustle while this deal closed because if this one didn't close, I wanted to have many other deals in my pipeline. Always be cautious and keep your pipeline full of deals so you don't have to worry about not getting paid! Friday came and twenty minutes before closing, the title company called me and said my check was ready. I had to rush over and get it before they closed because of course I didn't want to wait till Monday to get paid! I barely made it right before they closed and I grabbed my check. I just sat back in my truck and stared at the check. I couldn't believe I actually did it and closed this deal for $8,200. I just kept looking at it with one of my close friends Donovan. I looked at him and that's when I knew I was never going back to struggling. I told him this is it and it's all the way up from here!

 Something about holding one of those bigger checks and realizing all your hard work paid off is just an amazing feeling. You will never have a greater feeling than that of accomplishing something for which you worked so hard. I strive for this feeling all the time now because of how euphoric it is. Every deal I've done after this one I still feel the same. Keep working hard and always work towards the feeling, not just the material things! Anything is possible if you work hard enough.

What did the deal do for me, and what doors have opened since? When I talk about what this particular deal did for me and what doors it opened, I'm talking about the opportunities it created along the journey and this deal just topped it off. I was working hard the whole time but you know people only love seeing results. They don't care about the talk, they care about the walk! And now I was finally walking the walk. Nobody believed or knew what I was doing until I started showing results and actual progress in my real estate journey. I was growing up from newbie to knowing something and doing deals. I was getting more creative and making deals work every day I could. The journey up until that deal was incredible. I grew more than I ever thought I would, and learned more than I ever thought possible, too. After completing this deal and everybody on social media saw me, word got around about me. People knew who I was and viewed me as competition. I also started getting a lot of haters which wasn't bad. It meant I was doing something right. I was feeling good because all my hard work was paying off and everybody was noticing. My family supported me and they all congratulated me. I was getting affirmations that I was on the right path and everything just felt like it was falling into place. My team started giving me more tips on how to close deals and I just never felt closer to them than now. I think once I did that deal they all took me seriously. In fact, everybody around me started to take me seriously. And I was 100% serious about succeeding in this industry. I had a lot of people doubt me when I first started but once the checks and the results began showing, they knew I wasn't playing around. I think that's a really good feeling when people finally take you seriously and you feel great about where you are in your life. I didn't care about proving people wrong, that's not why I started doing what I did. I went into real estate as a way of gaining financial freedom. I knew exactly what I wanted to accomplish when I initiated my journey and nothing was going to stand in my way. No matter how many haters I had or people who wanted to see me fail, I was going to succeed no matter what got in my way. And that's exactly how I want each and every one of you to think. No matter what gets in your way or the hard times you go though, always succeed. Don't let anything or any person stop you. Since the day I told myself that I've been better off ever since. Where I started and where I am today are entirely different places. in fact, they are different worlds. I knew I would be successful one day but never thought I would do it before everybody else in my class, friends and older family. I'm glad I started when I did and I'm glad I am where I am and I'm very excited to see what the future will bring.

After that deal was competed I met a lot of new people doing real estate and other businesses. A little bit later I met a guy named Carlos Reyes. Super great guy and we connected over real estate because he saw the things I was doing. We started speaking almost every day and became great friends. He also introduced me to his side business of medical commodities. We talked more about it and I got involved so now I've got and extra stream of income. Which wasn't possible without knowing Carlos who I met through real estate and the deals I was doing. Everything happens for a reason and I knew I was meant to meet him. One way or another I knew I would've met him. That's just one example of the blessings I received from working hard and doing the deals I did.

Don't sit back and let other people take over. Take control of your life and conquer your market. If I can accomplish everything I have and jump into the real estate business at 18 years old, so can you! Anything is possible if you are willing to work hard enough and just hustle. I'm blessed to be where I am today and I hope each and every one of you get to where you're going. I hope you all become successful and own the world. Good luck, everybody. I believe in all of you!

**Chapter Seven**

**How to Make Money in Real Estate at Any Age**

**"Real estate investing even on a very small scale remains a true and tried means of building an individual's cash flow and wealth." Robert Kiyosaki**

This whole chapter is going to be about some basic ways to make money in real estate like driving for dollars, notes, direct mail, bandit signs and Craigslist. But I will also talk about a more secret way to make more money that they don't teach you. I will go into a few other ways that they don't teach you and different techniques you can start using today. There are so many ways to become successful in real estate. There are so many different avenues and roads you can take to become a millionaire. You can become an agent and list homes for a living and make well over a million dollars a year. I know many Realtors doing six figures monthly. How would your life change if you could produce six figures for your family every month, every year for the next ten years?

Realtors make their money by taking a percentage from the total sales price. They typically take 3%. It's not hard math, you get a $1 million house under contract for somebody who wants to sell, you market the property then close. You take the 3% and before your brokerage takes their cut, you get a check for $30,000. Now imagine if you did that 5 times a month and closed on them every single month. Five closed deals a month, $1 million per deal, is $150,000 a month in straight commissions. This is one of the longer routes to take because you do need to get a license to list homes on the market. You can grow very quickly this way and make some big commissions, but just like any other road in real estate, it takes time and effort to become the best. You could be an investor and flip homes for a living and make a million dollars very easily. Heck, you could make six figures from one flip if you position yourself correctly.

    Another road you could go down is once you collect a good amount of money from flipping, take that money and invest it into apartments, multifamily or commercial buildings to rent out. Apartments are the end game for most people because they provide passive income every month that requires no action on your part. Just set yourself up properly in the beginning of the deal and the cash will flow every month. When you first buy a few apartment buildings or even duplexes, you must take care of the place and deal with tenants. But once you acquire a few more buildings and start building a substantial cashflow every month, you can outsource to a property management company and they will take care of everything. You could literally just collect checks every month while you sit back at home or while visiting the world.

    Realistically, this should be the end game for most real estate entrepreneurs because it requires the least effort after the beginning and can make you some big bucks every month for the rest of your life. Then when you get old you can either sell the buildings and cash out crazy because they will most likely be paid off and you'll have amazing equity, or you can hand them down to your kids to manage them while they send you some checks to live off. Heck, you can even just be a bird dog for the rest of your life and still do very well and even make a million bucks in five years. A bird dog is someone that finds deals for investors to buy and they get a small cut. I know many bird dogs that get many checks every month from the leads they sent to investors. They aren't huge checks but 10 checks a month for $1k-$2k consistently adds up very quickly.

Last but not least, you could just put properties under contract and sell them to investors and make a million dollars. It's like a bird dog but a lot more work is put into it such as viewing the property, negotiating, researching and making contracts. It's more work but the reward can be so much greater because you control the numbers and can control your profit. You can put all these homes under contract with little to none of your own money and make $100k a month easily within five years. Even within two years. You've just got to be hungry enough to want it. One of my close business friends, Carlos Reyes, did $300k in real estate in one month. All from finding properties, getting them under contract then selling them to the other investors for a hefty profit. I think aside from being a bird dog, this is one of the easiest and fastest ways to grow your wealth in real estate. That $300k was also made with zero money out of pocket besides marketing which you don't need to spend a lot of money on.

This big check for $300k didn't entirely change his life but it did change his company and push them onto the next level doing bigger and better things. That's the greatest thing about real estate: one deal can change your life. One deal can pull you from the struggle to doing very well. One deal will take you from zero to hero. Did you know the average time it takes to become a millionaire in real estate is five years? That's the average amount of time it takes to make a million dollars. If you were promised a million bucks in five years, would you hustle every day now? Nothing in this life is guaranteed but numbers don't lie. I like those odds and I'll go for it. Some of the richest people in the world earned their money from real estate. Everybody knows that if you want to become wealthy then invest in real estate because people will always need a place to live. Real estate will never go away. Investing in land is the best investment you can make because it never goes away. You can't get rid of earth. Warren Buffet, third richest guy in the world because of real estate/ Berkshire Hathaway. Drew Scott from "Property Brothers" the TV show, Realtor worth ten million. So, if all these people are becoming rich and wealthy in real estate why do you work a 9-5 and expect your boss to make you rich? Mostly everybody that starts out in real estate works for somebody else but it's not like a 9-5. It's a business, a partnership. You work with partners, people you actually like and enjoy being around. Not working around a bunch of people you hate, can't stand and didn't choose. Normally, when you join a real estate team it's with people who all have the same thing on their mind, being successful and winning. Not just a paycheck.

    Your whole team will be on the same level and will be working hard together because they know they will get further as a team. Once you start doing better with your team and start stacking that liquid capital you can venture on your own which can happen very soon after starting. I would say within 2-3 years you can break away from that beginning team and start your own doing your thing with your own LLC. That's when you run your business and can have that financial freedom which all these people I mentioned have done. Or if you're like Drew Scott you can even start your own TV show. Whatever path you take in real estate it will be the fastest way to work for yourself and gain financial freedom in my opinion. Facts support that you can be a millionaire in five years and the business will never go away. There may be low times but there are also very high times, the same as in any business. The only other thing that is staying this strong, perhaps, is marketing and car sales. The best bet for any person growing up and not knowing what to do, is invest in real estate and gain some experience in this field.

Then you can make enough money to launch any other business you want to start and really venture off to do whatever you want! Just because you're in one business doesn't mean you need to be tied down and not create several other businesses. Millionaires need at least seven income streams to hold that millionaire status. Whatever you do, be strong and courageous enough to take that first step and work for yourself. You've got this!

Here are a few basic ways you can find deals in real estate in any market you are in. Also, finding buyers and sellers in your local market. Starting off in real estate you are going to be filled with millions of questions. I know I certainly was. You're going to be curious where to go, how to do it and why you are doing it. You want to know the results about everything and all kinds of facts.

Trust me you'll never stop learning. You'll keep learning new things every day as a real estate entrepreneur. Every day, every person I see who enters the field and thinks they can do this will ask all the big dogs how they do it. While you should help everybody you can, most of these guys won't tell you the real truth about the business because this is why they are so big: they know the secret. Why would they give it away for free? Most of these "gurus" will charge you to know the real truth and all the secrets of becoming successful and making the most money. But most likely starting out as a young or inexperienced real estate entrepreneur you probably have little to zero funds, so buying education and knowledge is out of the picture. Starting out with no money is hard but in no way impossible. What you want to do is find as many real estate meetings as you can, join as many online groups as possible and the best thing you could do is find a mentor. This will be the fastest way for you to get knowledge for free and grow the fastest. The best thing I ever did was find a mentor. He helped me grow so fast and gave me so much knowledge. If I had to put a price tag on the knowledge he gave me and how much it's worth to me, it would easily be over a million dollars. I will forever be in debt to him. Thank you, Andrew, for everything you've done for me.

But starting out you will know nothing about anything. Like what's legal and what's not legal, where do I get contracts, what do I do once I get a house under contract. It's fine, everybody starts out somewhere but most start out with little to no knowledge. But like I said join everything real estate related you can and you can find a lot of free information. Take notes on everything you find because you might have to refer to it later down the road. Every bit of information you can back up by facts is useful information that you can use in your arsenal. Every tool you have is one more way to get a leg up over your competition and a better chance you have of succeeding. Joining real estate groups and meetings can be very useful and something you can use to your advantage.

If you're just starting out one of the very important things you'll need is buyers. You'll need people to buy your deals once you come across one. The scariest thing is having a property under contract and not being able to sell it or having to back out. No worries, even if you have zero buyers and you have a good deal, somebody will always buy it. Most of the times at these real estate meetings there will be plenty of buyers looking for more good deals. This will be a great time to network and get to know the buyer. Then find out everything he looks for in a property like area, price, condition, all the good stuff. Then you can get their contact info and boom you've got a solid buyer to rely on once you get deals.

People always underestimate the value of a good face to face meeting rather than a phone call. This would also be a good time to try and find a mentor that will feed you knowledge about real estate. Go to as many of these meetings in your area as you can. If you are wholesaling houses, which is the best choice when first starting out, you can find other wholesalers and work on deals together. Co-wholesaling is the best because it's way easier than regular wholesaling and you can co-wholesale a lot of deals in a month. It's very simple because you can just find a deal then co-wholesale with somebody who has a buyer that can close quickly if you don't have a buyer. Or you can have a bunch of good buyers and have somebody bring you a deal to close on. Typically, you split the profits with the person 50/50 but hey a $10,000 split in half is still a really good payday. But you want to try and spend your time wisely on both things, buyers and sellers. That way you can close by yourself and keep the full fee for yourself instead of co-wholesaling. Of course, you can be strong in one area and do many co-wholesale deals. You can grow your buyers' list very fast by going to those real estate meetings, lunch meet ups, being active in Facebook real estate pages and much more. You can find buyers on local Facebook real estate pages by just saying you're looking for buyers because you have deals. Also by posting Craigslist ads saying you buy houses. This will bring in many buyers and maybe a few sellers! Once you get into a Facebook real estate group you will quickly learn who are the big dog buyers in your area/market. Always try to be friends and get to know the big dogs because chances are you may be selling a deal to them one day and it's good to know them closely. You can also call those bandit signs you see everywhere in your town. Most of the time it's mainly other wholesalers posting those signs but sometimes it's actual real buyers looking for good deals to close on themselves.

Bandit signs are those signs you see everywhere that say "we buy houses cash" or something along those lines. Get to know those numbers and become familiar with them. Call all the new ones you see and let everybody know you are buying in that area. You gotta make people think you are the big dog in that area. Fake it til you make it! Now there are going to be a lot of fake/new wholesalers that you call. Because bandit signs are the cheapest and easiest way to get your number out to the public. Since there are going to be a lot of fakes out there, call anyway to find out how many deals they are doing and if you can make money together. More people on your team, the better chances you have at making money. Follow up with these people every few weeks with a text to see if you can help them or co-wholesale any deals with them. If they are a buyer, great, add them to your list and keep pushing forward. Finding buyers is pretty easy but finding sellers is the real tricky part. Good leads are hard to find because they require prodigious amounts of effort and time. The good solid deals. But there's no secret to getting deals, just hard work and hustling. The truth is most mentors or "gurus" will say that you can make $30k-$60k in 90 days or something like that. Which is very true, though this doesn't happen easily. It does take a lot of hustle and dedication. Don't expect to work 5-10 hours a week and make that kind of crazy cash. It doesn't happen with just a few phone calls or emails. Maybe once you get good enough and people bring you deals, but freshly starting out, it won't happen. So, before you go into real estate be ready for some hard work and some long days. If you want that six figure a month income, you gotta be willing to work hard and not give up. Your first deal might not come for a few months but that's okay! My first deal took six months but I wasn't hustling to my full capacity. Looking back now I could've hustled a lot harder and got the deal sooner but I didn't. I was still in high school so my schooling was in the way which slowed me down. But if you're willing to hustle and work hard here's something you can do to start working towards that first deal. Like I said before, Craigslist ads are a good way to market for both buyers and sellers. A lot of good seller leads on Craigslist. These are the old people that just want to sell their old crappy home. But be cautious because there are a lot of people who watch these ads every minute of every day praying for a good deal. What you gotta do to stand out is setup Craigslist searches. If you don't know what these are and how to set them up, look on YouTube. They are very simple yet very effective. You basically setup these keyword searches and then as soon as somebody posts something matching your keywords, they send you an email.

As soon as you get these emails open them up and call them ASAP. Chances are you are the first one to call and hopefully the first one to set up an appointment and get the deal. This a very good and free way to get leads. It just requires a lot of hustle! Out of all the ways to find leads and deals, pick a few and master them. Don't dip and dabble trying to do every single one of these daily. Work on just a few of them and slowly start to do the rest. Once you master a few you can start making that cash and slowly engage in all the other ways to make deals happen. Trust me over time it will happen! I promise!

Now, here are one or two secret ways I'll teach on how to find deals and get your first deal. These are based on my experiences finding deals, and will help you in trying to figure out what works best in your market. There are so many ways to find deals and solid seller leads. Many gurus and mentors will preach that direct mail and bandit signs work the best. Some will champion other methods. But what works the best is what works for you and the area surrounding you. Sounds pretty simple, huh? Most people do not understand this very simple way of working. You must do what works the best in your market. Because the truth is, not every single method will work well in your market. Bandit signs will not work in areas where code enforcement is very strict and they take your signs down as soon as you put them up. So, what do you do when you realize that the strategies your "mentor" taught you don't work where you live? My first tip to you would be to get a mentor in your common market. If you're in California, don't listen to somebody that's in Colorado or New York. The market is different, and chances are all the things this person is saying will work for you, most likely will not work for you. Your mentor should already be teaching you what works in your market; if he isn't, go and try everything. That's right, try everything! How are you going to know what works If you haven't tried it? When I first started out I listened to what everybody said online and tried all the basic things that everybody else was doing. Or everybody was saying to do things that cost way too much upfront money.

 My advice to you is don't listen to what everybody says is the best way to find deals. Go out and test every single way to see what works. Some ways you may not be able to afford and some ways you can't do because of other reasons. But out of all the ways you can find deals, go out and try them for yourselves. You can talk all day long but taking action is what really matters. You can write down all these ideas about what you think will work and your blueprint to get the deals, but it doesn't matter unless you back it by action. It doesn't matter if you have an idea, it matters if you go out and test this idea and see if it works. It doesn't matter if you fail, every time you fail means you're one step closer to that deal. Never spend more time than you need to planning an idea before you actually test the idea yourself. You can always come back to the idea. Just think of something, create a plan then take some action. If you go out and try some way to market and it doesn't show instant results, don't worry. Rethink who you approached and try again.

 The key to making a certain marketing strategy work is consistency. Just because you did it a few days and saw little to no results doesn't mean it doesn't work. It just means you need to spend a little more time on this strategy. There are a few things you can do that work well but do cost quite a bit of money. Like direct mail marketing. I'm sure you've heard this more than once before. Everybody will preach that this is the best and maybe the only way to get seller leads. Direct mail is just the junk mail fliers you get every month for restaurants and businesses. But it's a custom flier that says "I want to buy your house" and they are sent to a specific group of people, either out of state owners, people behind on taxes or people who have owned their home for a long period of time. This is a great way to market because chances are these sellers are motivated if they own an out of state house and probably tired of being a landlord or they are behind on their taxes. While this is a great way to market for leads, this is also a pricey way that I would not recommend until you do a few big deals. A good campaign for direct mail will cost about $3k-$10k to see real results. The reason it costs so much is because you're mailing to over 1,000 people every month for about five to seven months. The key with this is consistency as well. You can't just mail somebody a letter for a month, it's typically gotta be for around five to seven in order to see results and close deals. Don't listen to what people say and invest all the money you have into this strategy if you only have $500-$1000. It's not worth it and probably just a waste of your money. Instead, save that money and use it to survive or put it into the next secret strategy I'm going to tell you about.

I'm going to tell you about a way that I find deals every week and many, many leads. This actually isn't even secret, it's just the fact that nobody is doing it that makes it so effective. This won't work in every market but it sure will work in most. The thing I do that brings me the most leads and the most deals, is a combination of driving for dollars, door knocking and calling Realtor signs. Driving for dollars is just getting in your vehicle and driving neighborhoods and looking for vacant and distressed houses. Once you come across a vacant or distressed looming property, you write down the address and try to search the owner once you get back home. You can skip trace them and find the current address and phone number and you can also send them a letter saying you want to buy the property. Whatever you do, your goal is to get in touch with the owner and buy the property. Very simple and tons of people do it. This is a great way to get leads and most likely they will be motivated because you're bringing up the fact that they have an unwanted property. They might have tenants and hate being a landlord and you come in by bringing a solution to buy the house.

While this is an effective strategy, you can make it so much more effective for every house you come across. Instead of just writing down the address, get out of your vehicle and knock on the door. I know this sounds scary but make sure you knock on the door the correct way and don't create any tension and you'll be fine. Nobody ever gets hurt door-knocking and nobody will just shoot you. Trust me it's safe. When you knock on the door, stand back far enough to give them space and always speak in a friendly manner. If they start acting kind of strange or raising their voice, just leave. You want to just introduce yourself and let them know who you are. Make sure to have a business card on you as well and let them know you pay about $500 for a referral. People love easy money.

Always end the conversation with a question or mention the easy $500. Just be friendly and let them know you are buying homes in the area. If nobody answers the door, make sure to have a flier of some sort or a simple sticky note saying you want to buy their house. So many people are afraid to even walk up to the door. You have a better chance of buying somebody's house if you get in front of them and show them who you are. When they get a letter in the mail they don't know who you are, what you look like or anything about you. Being face to face is the best way to sell something. Emotions are higher and you're more likely to cave in. I've acquired so many leads and closed so many deals using this technique of just getting out and talking to the homeowner. My partner who does the same thing consistently closes deals every month from this method. Also, target a neighborhood you know investors will buy in, not just a neighborhood close to you. Get used to the neighborhood and talk to everybody. If you just get out of the car and door knock all the distressed homes and tell everybody you're buying homes, you will get so many direct deals and leads. Even if they don't want to sell dirt cheap you can also refer them to a Realtor you know and you can get a nice referral fee from them. Make sure you have a good Realtor on your team. They make the difference! Also, when you are in the area, call and text all Realtor signs nearby. Try to offer seller financing or offer a fair cash offer. Since they are selling homes in that area you can tell them to let you know when they get pocket listings/off market deals where the sellers need to sell fast. Make Realtors your best friend and I promise you will do more deals! None of this works unless you take action. So, get up and go make it happen!

The basic and organic ways are the best ways to find the most profitable deals. Organic ways of finding seller leads are the basic ways to find deals. It's before all the online marketing and direct mail happened. It's the grass roots where you have to hustle and bust your butt to get deals. They are where you find the most direct deals and the most profitable. They are by no means the easiest but they can be the most rewarding. It takes a lot of driving, talking, calling and just straight hustling. Some organic ways of finding sellers are Craigslist, driving for dollars, door knocking and bandit signs. Those are all the most basic ways to find deals. These are the grass roots of where it all happened. Before computers were around people actually went door to door asking if homeowners wanted to sell their home. They didn't send mass amounts of letters and market online. So, when everything else fails like direct mail and online marketing, the organic ways of finding deals will always work. These ways are what started the real estate business and doing deals and will always produce deals.

    Since everybody is getting into real estate lately, it makes it difficult for a fix and flip buyer to find direct deals. Direct deals are where the buyer is direct to the seller. Nobody is in between trying to resell the deal. This creates lots of problems as far as price because you can't renegotiate the price. Most buyers who want fix and flips want to be direct with the seller so if they need to negotiate a lower price or something comes up, they can handle it themselves and a lot easier. Way easier than dealing with a few people who are in the middle trying to resell the deal. Also, when multiple people get involved in the deal, the profit goes down because everybody is trying to get a cut and it slowly eats up the profit. Moreover, the price the seller gets is a lot smaller and oftentimes makes them unhappy, which can cause you to lose a deal and waste all the time you spent on it. So, if you get a deal directly on your own, you can maximize your profit by dealing directly with the seller and not having to worry about splitting your fee. Instead of splitting your $10,000 fee with two other people because you weren't direct, you can now keep that full $10k. That's a nice little payday. That's where the basic ways of getting a deal will play in your favor. And when you get some big money and spend it all on direct mail or getting leads online, you can do the basic ways and rack up a little cash in the meantime. Driving for dollars and door knocking require little to no money, just a vehicle with some gas. These ways will also remain the cheapest approaches to finding deals when you are tight on your budget or just beginning. This is something anybody at any age could do. Even successful Realtors go around and door knock now. People would prefer to just see your face and know who you are rather than searching for you online. Online does bring a lot of leads and everybody uses the Internet now, but there's nothing wrong with a little friendly face to face communication. I know this older lady Realtor in her sixties who door knocks and makes well over six figures per year. Also, bandit signs cost very little and just require some hustle to put them all out. You can get deals from this but they do cost money and can add up if you buy a lot of them. Of course, Craigslist is another free way where you can set appointments all day to see homes that local people are selling. This is a good way to get tons of experience talking with sellers and going to appointments. Craigslist is free and there are tons of deals on there. I've personally found a few deals even in the competitive Arizona market I'm in. So, Craigslist will most likely work in any market and there will be deals! You just gotta work hard and find them!

**Chapter Eight**

**Adapting & Changing in Different Situations/Survival**

"In order to attain the impossible, one must attempt the absurd."- Miguel De Cervantes

During your journey as an entrepreneur, you will face many different situations where you need to adapt to the circumstances and solve the problem. You must to be willing to do this for every problem you come across, and you will come across a lot. As an entrepreneur, this is something you must do in order to run your business smoothly and get over any obstacles you come across. Nobody ever said being an entrepreneur is easy but in the end, it is so worth the struggle. Every day is an adventure when you step outside the 9-5 life and jump into the entrepreneur life. You don't know what to expect and every day will be different. A lot of the days you will face some difficulties and must overcome them. When you work a 9-5 you rarely come across hard days, maybe your car will break down or you'll deal with a difficult customer but that's about it. Since you rarely come across these difficulties you don't really ever learn how to become stronger and overcome these obstacles. These people just know how to deal with occasional bumps in the road and continue to live. But you don't get stronger by just dealing with problems, you become stronger by tackling them and overcoming the obstacles. Waking up every day as an entrepreneur you will face an obstacle almost every day, so you will need to be strong enough to fight through them. You can't be soft headed and cry. You will need to man up and conquer your day because some days you will fight way harder than others and every day matters. But that's the fun and exciting part about being self-employed. You give up the easy 9-5 life for a hard, challenging yet rewarding lifestyle. It's also a 24/7 job. But no matter what comes your way just man up and always make sure you show up. That's the most important thing I've learned so far. If you don't show up, you won't even have a chance. Even if you think all odds are against you, always show up because you never know what will happen. There have been many times where I didn't feel like waking up, getting up or even showing up to events I knew I didn't have a chance at. But I still got up and went. The times where you really don't feel like going are the times where you need to go!

    Pushing yourself past the limits is when you ultimately change your life. You don't change your life by staying comfortable, you change your life by being incredibly uncomfortable. Something I realized was that when I get out of my environment I come up with some of my best ideas and improve the most. So, since I first realized that, I change up everything now. You never know what you could be missing out on if you just change up a few things you do every day. Every day I drive a different route, wake up different times, organize my day differently and just chance up everything so I can come across as many opportunities as possible. I'll even switch up the way my room is arranged and eat somewhere different every day. I'm always trying to get outside my comfort zone in order to get to that next level of success. I highly encourage you to do the same. Start off slowly by driving different ways to where you need to go or rearrange your living space. And always be doing new things in your business to facilitate growth.

Don't just do the things that make you comfortable and in a routine so to say. An example of this would be the day I woke up and decided to door knock 30 doors and get my business out there. I was very uncomfortable doing this and I made every excuse to not do it. It was too hot or I didn't have enough gas or I needed a haircut. I thought of it all! But I knew it would be good for me and I knew I would get some sort of leads or deals from it. I got dressed up and just drove to where I wanted to door knock. So long as I got there I would go do it. Once I parked and got ready to get out I just sat there scared and not wanting to go. It would be so easy just to go home and not do it. I'd never been so uncomfortable in my life. I was afraid of the rejection and getting the door slammed in my face. But I said this is for the future you and I promise you'll look back and be glad you did it. So, I just manned up and went. It was for the greater good and I thought about that the whole time I walked to each and every door.

This was a huge confidence obstacle for me. I know most people can't just walk up to random doors and start talking. It's nerve racking. Afterwards, though, I had a few leads and more people knew about me. When I was driving home, I felt way more confident and just overall better about myself. After you do something you didn't think was possible you feel a lot different. I'm always out door knocking and speaking to everybody I can about my business. So, get out there no matter what and make those big moves that make you uncomfortable. Plow through those obstacles!

OK, let's talk about becoming an entrepreneur. What exactly is an entrepreneur? Google says an entrepreneur is a person who organizes and operates a business or businesses, taking on greater than normal financial risks in order to do so. This isn't just a job, it's a lifestyle. When you first start out quitting your job and becoming an entrepreneur most people will think this is just another job. They think they will just wake up, work and become successful. How wrong these people are! This is a life changing transformation. If your life doesn't change and you don't blow up when you become self-employed/entrepreneur then you aren't giving it your all and if you're not willing to give it your all, don't give anything at all. Be willing to wake up and give it your all. Always go to bed feeling that you gave the day everything you could and you will grow much faster. Going to bed feeling exhausted but fulfilled in doing everything you can in your business that day is the best feeling. So many people over estimate what they can do in a day. You can't build yourself a new world in a day. While you can do a lot in one day, you can't build an entire successful business in just 24 hours. Giving it all you can for ten to fifteen hours a day Monday through Saturday and maybe a few hours on Sunday will grow your business so fast. Most people only work on their business a few hours a day and expect it to become successful in four weeks. But the more effort and time you put into it, your business will show results a lot sooner.

Here are some examples of situations you will come across in real estate and in any business in general. There will be "almost" deals you will come across, but you need to keep moving forward. It will get hard and it be difficult for a while. You will come across a lot of deals you think will work, but then won't in the end. It's hard on the mind to fail so many times before succeeding. One thing that was the hardest for me was failing a whole bunch of times until I got it right and succeeded. Before, I was always that person that if I didn't see immediate results, I quit. That's just the way I was raised really. I was raised to do things that were the easiest. I wasn't raised around successful businessmen who taught me to struggle through the hard times and succeed. I was raised in a middle class environment around people who worked 9-5. Nobody ran a business in my family except my grandparents. I didn't grow up around these people and by the time I was old enough to know what business was, their business had slowed down and they were much older. They were already establishing enough to not have to work as hard anymore or struggle. They had it figured it out and running well. Once you get to a certain spot in your business, you won't go backwards anymore, just forward, unless there is a crash in the market or something extremely bad happens to your business. However, even if something bad happens in your business like the market crashes or money stops coming in, you've got to remain calm and keep progressing. The last thing you want to do is quit when the times get tough. Figure out the problem when one occurs and overcome it.

The best thing you can do is prepare for almost every scenario that could happen and figure out how you would get through each scenario. That way, when you run into one of those problems, you know exactly how to handle it and overcome it. This will be the best thing you can do because it will give you an edge over your competition. But you can't prepare for everything so it's best just to be on high alert. Because chances are when a crash happens, it will affect everybody's business. All those other people will spend time freaking out, worrying what to do next and just be in a complete frenzy. In the meantime, you're cool and calm because you know exactly what to do and how to do everything. All the time your competition will spend freaking out, you'll spend rebuilding and be back in business way before the rest. Therefore, giving you enough time to get ahead and advance further than everybody else was before. A perfect example in real estate for me would be dealing with lack of funds. This is a very common problem to deal with in real estate. With any business in general, in the beginning you will need to figure out how to make every penny count and go as far as you can.

Most of the time when you start a business you will either be struggling or have some cash to invest in yourself. Either way if you have a cash or not, you must be careful with every dollar you have. Don't be one of those people who invests every dollar they have into one idea without anything to back it up. I would never invest everything I have into just one idea without calculating all my risks. Either way, risking all your funds is way too risky and especially just starting out, because if you lose all your funds, you'll feel discouraged and quit. Which you do not want to do! Do not go back to your 9-5 ever again once you have become self-employed. But when you do first start your business, map out a plan of what you need for your business and what costs will be recurring every month. Then you can set a goal for yourself on how much you need to make to pay for all costs then profit. And if you start a business with money on your side, put it away and only spend it on what's necessary, because when you started working for yourself, you probably quit your day job and have no more income. Once you spend a dollar, that dollar is not coming back until you start succeeding and your business starts producing cash flow. You'll have to just be cautious and careful with all the money you have. If you need to invest some money in your business, factor in all risks and make a calculated purchase/move. Only make moves when you feel you will benefit and do good from it. You always need to be going outside your comfort zone but you don't need to do so with your funds. Always push yourself harder both mentally and physically but just take care of your cash. Don't make any big moves unless you're almost 100% sure it will pay off. If there's a big possibility for failure, be prepared on how to recover and bounce back from it.

It will be hard and you will be stressed out a lot at first. But don't worry, better times are coming. Being an entrepreneur is all about taking risks, just be smart and take well calculated ones. No need to be silly and lose all your money. Don't, however, let the fear of losing everything hold you back from taking big risks to push you forward. Be willing to pull the trigger when you feel the time is right and the investment is worth it. The only thing worse than foolishly wasting your money, is wasting your time on people. The best decision I made was to invest my time only in people who deserve it. When you start growing as a businessperson and developing as a person in general, money will come more easily. When you first start, money is all you're thinking about so you can live a nice life and enjoy the finer things. But once you start to make more money, you realize it doesn't fulfill you like you thought it would. I wish everybody could become rich and successful to realize that's not what's it's all about. Jim Carey once said this: "I hope everybody could get rich and famous and will have everything they ever dreamed of, so they will know that it's not the answer." Jim Carey was broke before he was in his first big movie *Dumb and Dumber*. He put a check in his wallet for $10 million and dated it for five years ahead. He said, "I'm going to do it." Just before the date expired on the check, he found out he was going to make $10 million on *Dumb and Dumber*, which was a very funny – and very successful -- movie. Point being, he was dedicated and he knew exactly what he wanted. He took the risk and became successful.

Another great example of taking risks is Elon Musk. Most people that read this book will know who this man is. Elon Musk is the creator of Tesla, SpaceX and PayPal. He was the second entrepreneur in Silicon Valley, California. He saw an opportunity of the computer and Internet evolving in the market. He saw that the Internet was going to stick around when everybody thought it was just a fad. Elon created PayPal because up until that moment, people were not sending money online, everything was still all cash. He is one of the few inventors of this time. He invented PayPal which is one of the best ways to send money electronically besides the bank and such. Elon filled a hole we had and a problem we had in the new and upcoming market. The Internet would grow into something more than anybody would ever imagine. PayPal is huge now and worth over $49 billion. When you add value to people's lives and solve problems, that will be the best invention and be the most successful. But Elon took a massive risk after PayPal. He was always thinking ahead. In the beginning, Elon made $180 million from PayPal, he then invested $100 million into SpaceX, $70 million in Tesla and $10 million into Solar City. He invested all the money he had into those companies because he believed in them so strongly. He had literally all his money invested so he had to borrow rent! But look at how his investments are paying off now.

  I would only tell you to take big risks like this when you feel 100% confident in your decision and you also have plans just in case it doesn't work. This scenario would be sink or swim. Pretty much burning all bridges so you have to learn to make it work no matter what. Always be careful about what risks you take and be willing to take calculated risks. I've seen fear kill more people than being safe has. Don't be afraid to take the risks and you will survive. Business is a survival world and you must learn to survive no matter what. It's something you'll learn once you get through more of your journey. I didn't learn to take big risks until I got more into my journey and realized that being an entrepreneur is all about taking risks. I also learned that being in business means doing things you wouldn't have before and living a life you never lived before. Being an entrepreneur is way different than working as an employee 9-5. You'll think differently because you have to figure out how to get that check. Checks won't come in every week like a 9-5 and you won't always work the same hours every day and every week. It's not going to be an easy journey but I can assure you that it will be well worth it. You will grow more than you ever thought was possible because you are more powerful than you will ever understand. Use the power God gave you and go out and hustle. No matter what obstacles get in your way or people that judge you. Just keep going along your journey and remember to do what's right. In the end the only thing you'll regret is not starting sooner. Keep hustling and you can achieve anything!


The obstacles will help grow your business and help you blow up in your market. The sooner you realize to appreciate all the no's and rejections, the faster you'll grow your business into a huge enterprise. I just want to say that this journey will be hard. It will require a lot of late nights studying and perfecting your business. Long nights where you can't sleep because you're stressing on how to make enough money survive the next week. You will be doing things that most people will not understand and most people will not support because they will think you're crazy. They will ask you why work so hard every single day, why you work 10+ hours every day sometimes for $0. Why work so hard when you can just get a 9-5 job and receive a paycheck every week? They say it's so much easier to work the 9-5 job, get a paycheck every week, collect Social Security when you retire, then buy a nice house and car. Everybody will question everything you do without understanding the concept of being self-employed. I truly believe the only people who will understand your journey will be other people that are on the same path as you and encountering the same things. Your parents will support you for a while then kind of lose hope if you don't show some real money or proof. You will think some of your closest friends will be by your side, but truth is most of your friends will come and go. I've had a lot of friends I thought would stay by my side no matter but when things got tough for me they left me and I was all alone except for the people who stuck by my side no matter what. I dare you to look at the people around you. Your closest friends and family. Look at who is there before you start your entrepreneur journey and who stays when you struggle and who leaves. Then look at the people who try to come back when you are successful. I guarantee the same people who were there before you started the journey will not be the ones who are there with you when you end, with the exception of the ones who will stick by your side the rest of the way. All the people who stay with you during all the hard times, the struggling and success, the people who see it all will be the ones that are meant to be by your side as you grow even bigger and develop into an even better person.

    I soon realized after I started my journey that it's not about how many friends you have, it's about the quality of friends you have and the quality of the family that surrounds you. Out of all the friends I had before, only three of them actually stuck around and became my best friends. I want to give thanks to my best friends Donovan, Bernardo and Trevor. They stuck by my side when nobody else would and took care of me until I started becoming successful and earning some money for myself. Whenever I needed help or money to keep going, they kept me afloat. These three people are the people I trust with my life and the reason I keep pushing hard every single day. I work hard every single day because I owe my life to these guys. I owe everything I have to these three people. They were there even when everybody else had left. I constantly show my gratitude by giving it everywhere as much as I can, and helping them anyway I can.

    A few other people who were there for me was my mom and dad. No matter what I went through, no matter how down I was, I can always count on them to lift my spirits and push me out the next day. They never gave up on me and they always provided support for my business. My mom and dad always provided a shoulder I could cry on when things started to get a little tough and I didn't think it was going to happen for me. They always gave me the best life possible even when money was tight. We were never a rich family but that never mattered because I had all the love and support anybody could ever ask for. I have mainly created my businesses around the sole fact that one day I will be able to provide them the life that they provided for me and make all their dreams come true and take them wherever they want to go. I love you, Mom and Dad. Thank you for everything you've ever done for me.

    The purpose of all this is to say that when you find somebody that is very special and sticks by your side no matter what, please hold onto that person very tightly and don't let go. Treat these people like kings and queens and they will never let you down or ever leave your side. I hope you guys find the best success along your journey into your entrepreneurial world and I hope this book has helped you in some way start or create an even better business.

The end. The journey will continue. This is my first but not my last book.

www.ingramcontent.com/pod-product-compliance
Lightning Source LLC
Chambersburg PA
CBHW051330170526
45166CB00002B/757